NATIONAL GEOGRAPHIC

Glacier and Waterton Lakes National Parks Road Guide

THE **ESSENTIAL** GUIDE FOR MOTORISTS

by
Thomas Schmidt

D1550657

One of the world's largest nonprofit scientific
and educational organizations, the National
Geographic Society was founded in 1888 "for the
increase and diffusion of geographic knowledge."
Fulfilling this mission, the Society educates and
inspires millions every day through its magazines,
books, television programs, videos, maps and
atlases, research grants, the National Geographic
Bee, teacher workshops and innovative classroom
materials. The Society is supported through
membership dues, charitable gifts, and income
from the sale of its educational products. This
support is vital to National Geographic's mission
to increase global understanding and promote
conservation of our planet through exploration,
research, and education.For more information,
please call 1-800-NGS-LINE (647-5463), or write
to the following address:

National Geographic Society
1145 17th Street N.W.
Washington, D.C. 20036-4688
U.S.A.

Contents

"Get off the track at Belton Station, and in a few moments you will find yourself in the midst of what you are sure to say is the best care-killing country on the continent—beautiful lakes derived straight from glaciers, lofty mountains steeped in lovely nemophila-blue skies and clad with forests and glaciers, mossy, ferny waterfalls in their hollows, nameless and numberless, and meadowy gardens abounding in the best of everything…Give a month at least to this precious reserve. The time will not be taken from the sum of your life. Instead of shortening, it will indefinitely lengthen it."

—John Muir, 1901

"No words can describe the grandeur and majesty of these mountains, and even photographs seem hopelessly to dwarf and belittle the most impressive peaks."

—George Bird Grinnell, 1901

"I wouldn't trade one square mile of Glacier for all the other parks put together."

—Ernie Pyle

How to Use This Guide

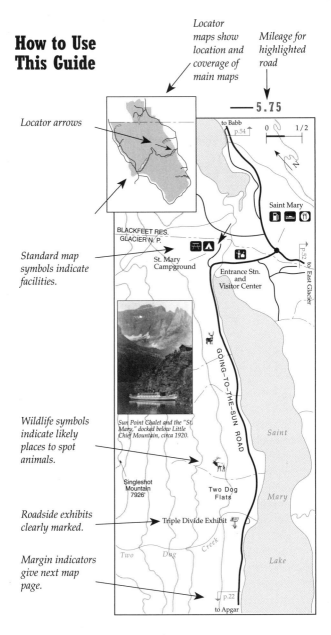

Locator maps show location and coverage of main maps

Mileage for highlighted road

— 5.75

Locator arrows

Standard map symbols indicate facilities.

Wildlife symbols indicate likely places to spot animals.

Roadside exhibits clearly marked.

Margin indicators give next map page.

to Babb
p.54

0   1/2

N

Saint Mary

to East Glacier
p.52

BLACKFEET RES.
GLACIER N. P.
St. Mary
Campground

Entrance Stn.
and
Visitor Center

GOING-TO-THE-SUN ROAD

Sun Point Chalet and the "St. Mary," docked below Little Chief Mountain, circa 1920.

Saint

Singleshot
Mountain
7926'

Two Dog
Flats

Mary

Triple Divide Exhibit

Two   Dog   Creek

Lake

p.22
to Apgar

- Key map inside front cover gives page numbers for road maps.
- Map features and commentary run side by side.
- Maps generally in sequence east-west, south-north. Page numbers for adjoining maps are given in map margins. Or refer to locator maps or key maps.
- This book is a guide for motorists, not hikers or other backcountry users, who will find topo-graphic maps and trail guides essential.

Carved by Ice

EASILY RANKING among the most spectacular and impressive natural preserves in North America, Glacier and Waterton Lakes National Parks combine roughly 1,800 square miles of rugged peaks, glacially carved valleys, deep mountain lakes, and splendid waterfalls. The parks are home to mountain goats and bighorn sheep, black bears and grizzlies, wolves, elk, moose, deer, and an abundance of other animals that fly, swim, or scurry through the area's forests, prairies, and lofty crags.

The spectacular mountain scenery that makes up Glacier and Waterton is the result of a geologic process that began more than 1.5 billion years ago. Back then, this part of the continent lay along the shifting coast of a primordial sea. Rain, streams, and rivers swept sand, silt, and limy mud from slopes to the north, east, and south and deposited them in layers along the coast and across the seabed. Over hundreds of millions of years, these sediments grew to a thickness of 3 to 5 miles and preserved within themselves ripple marks and mud cracks that can be seen today. The accumulated weight caused the ocean floor to sag and also changed the deposits into limestone, dolomite, siltite, and argillite.

The bottom portion of these rock layers make up today's mountains, but they originally rested roughly 40 miles west of their present location. One very slow

Welcome to Forsyth Central
You checked out the following items:

1. National Geographic Glacier and Waterton Lakes National Parks road guide : the essential guide for motorists
   Barcode: 39872001299020 Due: 6/4/2019

FORSYTH_CENTRAL
5/14/2019 4:27 PM
You were helped by Tony

but climactic event explains how the strata rose to the surface and moved across the land.

About 200 million years ago, the Earth's crustal plates began a slow collision along the western edge of what was then the North American continent. This collision slowly bulged the continent upward and elevated chains of mountains throughout the West, including the Rockies, which began to rise about 70 million years ago. The slab underlying Glacier and Waterton, however, performed an interesting trick. Breaking away from a slope to the west it slid slowly eastward for more than 40 miles. The cliffs that now rise from the plains on the east side of Glacier represent the leading edge of the slab, called the Lewis Thrust Fault Block. There, rock more than a billion years old rests atop layers a mere 60 to 70 million years of age.

For tens of millions of years, erosion carried off the upper layers of the thrust fault block. Eventually, the strata we see today was exposed, waiting only for the onset of the great ice ages to carve the peaks and ridges into their present forms.

One sees the effects of moving ice at almost every turn in either park. U-shaped valleys, cirques, and amphitheaters, hanging valleys, knife-edged arêtes, and moraines all attest to the work of great fingers of ice that began shaping these mountains at least 200,000 years ago. At least three times, scientists believe, the parks' mountains were burdened with ice that slowly bared the core of these peaks and then melted away. Today, some 30 to 40 new glaciers chisel away at Glacier's mountains. Relative dwarfs, they began forming several thousand years ago and are not remnants of ice age glaciers.

WHEN YOU STAND on the prairie east of the park and gaze at the mountains, you are looking at much more than an impressive assembly of rock and snow. As your eye traces the land from the grasses at your feet to the tops of the mountains, it skips across a wide spectrum of communities, or life zones, each of which is characterized by certain species of plants and animals. The higher you look, the shorter the growing season and the greater the amount of precipitation. The differences in climate are similar to those encountered while traveling from south to north at sea level. However, at sea level, one would have to cover roughly 3,100 miles to experience such a range of habitats.

Wetlands are dispersed throughout the park but support little life at higher elevations. Low-lying ponds, lakes, and marshy areas teem with plants, insects, fish, amphibians, waterfowl, and semi-aquatic mammals such as beaver and mink. They also attract large mammals, including moose, elk, and deer.

The Great Plains, once thick with herds of bison, end abruptly against the east slope of the mountains, but pockets of prairie extend into most of the eastern valleys. The food produced by the fescue, oatgrass, and wildflowers in these meadows supports elk and deer as well as a variety of small rodents, which in turn feed predators such as hawks and coyotes.

Farther up the slopes, groves of aspen mix with the grasses or spread over river valleys and creek beds. An assortment of berry bushes grows beneath the aspens and provides food for hares, rodents, and birds such as the ruffed grouse.

At higher elevations and on some north-facing slopes, the shorter growing season favors evergreen trees, which need not grow a new crop of leaves each year to photosynthesize. The wide bands of dark green forest that cover the middle slopes of the parks' mountains consist mainly of lodgepole, spruce, and fir. In the McDonald Valley on Glacier's west side, the moderating influence of moist Pacific air supports a deep forest of cedar and hemlock.

Between the deep forests and tree line lies the subalpine zone, where subalpine fir, Engelmann spruce and whitebark pine share a foothold with thickets of berry bushes and meadows of wildflowers, sedges, and grasses. In this zone live grizzly bears, bighorn sheep, wolverines, marmots, ground squirrels and, in the highest reaches, mountain goats.

The alpine tundra zone rises above timberline at the tops of the parks' highest mountains and resembles the vast, tree less areas of the Arctic. The few trees that survive the harsh climate hug the ground, twisting and bending around rocks that protect them from the wind. Tiny wildflowers grow in the thin soil and gravel among the rocks, and lichens cover the boulders and cliffs. Besides the mountain goat, ptarmigan, and pika (a tiny hare), few animals spend much time at this elevation.

C OMPARED WITH its natural history, the area's human history has passed in the blink of an eye. The area's first inhabitants fished the lakes and rivers and hunted buffalo (bison), elk, bighorn sheep, and deer. Some of their camps along the eastern slopes date back more than 8,000 years. About 1,000 to 1,500 years ago, some of the people moved west of the Continental Divide, venturing east just a few times a year to hunt buffalo on the plains. Why they moved west is not clear, but those who did were probably the ancestors of the Kootenai tribe.

In the early 1700s, the Kootenai acquired their first horses, a development that made it much easier to pack buffalo meat over the mountains. However, at about the same time, their neighbors to the northeast, the Blackfeet, acquired both the horse and the gun. This enabled the Blackfeet to dominate the entire eastern half of what are now the parks. The Blackfeet guarded the passes and largely succeeded in keeping out the west-side tribes.

The Rocky Mountain fur trade and the westward expansion of Anglo civilization laid low the Blackfeet by the end of the nineteenth century. Smallpox and illicit alcohol decimated them. Then miners found traces of minerals on their land and, in 1895, the Blackfeet sold the eastern half of what would become Glacier National Park to the U.S. government for $1.5 million. At about the same time, entrepreneurs were drilling oil wells in what would become Waterton Lakes National Park.

Meanwhile, conservationists such as George Bird Grinnell in the United States and F. W. Godsal in Canada tried to get their respective governments to preserve the lands as national parks. Fortunately for today's visitors, the mining and drilling claims soon proved worthless, and objections to creating the parks were swept aside. Waterton was set apart in 1895 as a forest reserve and later became a dominion park. In 1910, the United States established Glacier.

Although the Forty-ninth Parallel divides this magnificent territory between two nations, the park lands remain united ecologically. Partly because of this natural fusion and partly because of the long history of peace and friendship between the United States and Canada, the parks were combined in 1932 under the banner of Waterton-Glacier International Peace Park. It was the first of its kind in the world. Today, the park services of both countries strive to protect the ecosystem as a whole and to cooperate wherever possible in managing the preserve as if it did not lie in separate countries.

Travelers' Information

VISITOR CENTERS in both parks offer books, maps, brochures, videos, permits, and general information. Park naturalists and interpreters are on hand to answer any questions and to offer advice about roads, trails, and campgrounds. Some of the visitor centers offer interpretive videos or exhibits. Newspapers published by the parks list park services and seasonal schedules.

In Glacier, visitor centers are located at St. Mary, Logan Pass, and Apgar, near West Glacier. The Many Glacier Ranger Station offers many of the same services. All are open daily during the summer season (May–mid-Oct.), and Apgar is open on weekends November through March.

In Waterton, visitors can pick up information at: the Park Information Centre, across the main Waterton Road from the Prince of Wales Hotel; the Heritage Centre, on Waterton Avenue in the townsite; and the Park Administration Office, on Mount View Road in the townsite.

Entrance fees for Glacier are $20 per private vehicle, one permit good for seven days. People entering by other means (on bicycle, foot, or commercial bus) pay five dollars for the one-week permit. An annual permit for Glacier costs $25. A National Parks Pass runs $50 and grants entry for the bearer and passengers to all U.S. national parks for one year. Golden Age Passports, for U.S. residents age 62 or older, cost ten dollars; Golden Access Passports for the handicapped are free.

Entry fees in Waterton are complicated, with different rates for individuals, groups, senior citizens, and groups of seniors. Call or write for rates.

Correspondence and requests for information should be directed to: Headquarters, Glacier National Park, P.O. Box 128, West Glacier, MT, 59936 (tel 406-888-7800), *www.nps.gov/glac/home.htm*; or Information Bureau, Waterton Lakes National Park, Waterton Park, Alberta, TOK 2MO (tel 403-859-5133), *www.parks canada.gc.ca/waterton.*

Driving: Except where otherwise posted, speed limits in the parks are 45 mph (72 kph) in Glacier and 50 mph (80 kph) in Waterton. Some roads, particularly Glacier's North Fork Road, are unsuitable for RVs. Vehicle length and width restrictions are in effect for the Going-to-the-Sun Road. Contact Glacier National Park for current information on this major route.

Boating: Waterton does not require permits or fees to use boats in the park, but motors are restricted to Upper and Middle Waterton Lakes. Glacier enforces Montana state requirements for an annual state registration. Boats and motors of unlimited size are permitted on McDonald, Waterton, Sherburne, and St. Mary Lakes. Motors on Bowman and Two Medicine Lakes are limited to ten horsepower. On all other waters, only hand-propelled craft are allowed.

The swift, cold waters of the North Fork and Middle Fork Flathead River are popular among rafters. Several private companies run float trips; contact the park for a list of outfitters.

The waters of both parks can be very cold, and weather can change quickly from balmy to hazardous. In Glacier, the top cause of visitor deaths is drowning. Please be careful.

Fishing: Pike, whitefish, grayling, burbot, kokanee salmon, and several varieties of trout live in the parks' waters. Glacier requires neither fee nor permit to fish in its lakes, streams, and rivers. In Waterton, though, anglers age 16 and over must buy a license.

In both parks, regulations are designed to protect fish populations. For that reason, complicated rules that change from place to place apply. Copies of the regulations are available at entrance stations, visitor centers, and from park rangers.

Motorists gather near St. Mary for a day of touring in Glacier National Park, circa 1920.

Hiking: Driving is a pleasant way to get a quick overview of Glacier and Waterton, but it would be a shame to cruise through without stepping off the pavement. Short trails abound along the roads. Some of the trails have signs along the route to help identify and explain interesting points.

Also, park naturalists and interpreters lead hikes and strolls that range in length from about an hour to an entire day. These excellent interpretive hikes are conducted regularly from such centers as Lake McDonald, Many Glacier, St. Mary Lake, Goat Haunt, the Waterton Park Information Centre and Cameron Lake. The park publication *Nature with a Naturalist* provides a list of guided hikes in both parks. Some link up with excursion cruises on the parks' major lakes.

No permit is required for day hikes in either park, but some common-sense precautions are in order. Carry a trail map. Be prepared for sudden weather changes. Bring food and water for any but a very short hike. And please remember, this is bear country, so make plenty of noise in the woods to let them know you're coming and do not hike alone. The staffs of both parks stress how important it is to read and understand the free information about bears available to all visitors. Park naturalists and interpreters can also answer your questions about hiking and camping in bear country.

Horseback Riding: Guided trail rides are available in and adjacent to both parks. There are stables near Apgar, Lake McDonald Lodge, St. Mary, East Glacier, Many Glacier, and the Waterton Townsite. Each park has its own set of regulations and restrictions that apply to those who bring their own horses.

Bicycling: Bicyclists are welcome in both parks, but roads tend to be narrow with little or no shoulder. For this reason, sections of Going-to-the-Sun Road are closed to bicycles during some parts of the day in summer. In Glacier, bicycles are not allowed on trails.

Wheelchair Access: Both parks provide information about trails, trips, and other activities accessible to those with wheelchairs. Most visitor centers, some rest rooms, some ranger-led activities, and most roadside viewpoints are wheelchair accessible.

Also, some of the best roadside trails in the park can be navigated by wheelchair. These include the Trail of the Cedars, near Avalanche Campground, and a portion of the trail to the Hidden Lake Overlook at Logan Pass.

Wildlife: Glacier and Waterton Lakes parks provide one of North America's richest opportunities to appreciate wildlife. Among the major mammals, one can see elk, deer, moose, bison, mountain goats, bighorn sheep, black bears, grizzlies, and coyotes. Here too, but not so often seen, are mountain lions, lynx, bobcat, wolves, and wolverines. In addition to these and other mammals, the parks provide a home for a wide variety of birds. There are eagles, hawks, and osprey, great blue herons, harlequin ducks, pygmy owls, dippers, and calliope humming-birds. The Waterton Lakes lie at the intersection of the Central and Pacific flyways used by water-fowl of all description during the autumn and spring migrations.

Viewing wildlife should be done with care and sensitivity for the animals. Most will not tolerate the close approach of a human, and some will protect themselves when it occurs. Visitors are injured yearly and sometimes even killed by the parks' animals. Best rule: Stay in or near your car if you come across an animal close to the road. Give animals plenty of space.

Bears can be especially dangerous. Both parks publish sound advice on how best to avoid dangerous encounters with bears while camping, hiking, fishing or otherwise enjoying the outdoors.

Feeding animals, large or small, is forbidden!

Seasons: Although most roads in the parks close for the winter, one can usually count on driving to the head of Lake McDonald, Waterton Townsite, and Cameron Lake most of the year. However, the customs station at the U.S. and Canadian border along the Chief Mountain Highway closes in mid-September, effectively cutting that link between the parks. From October to May, travel between the parks is via Cardston, Alberta. Snow closes the rest of the roads beginning in October. The roads normally open again in May, although Going-to-the-Sun Road may not open to through traffic for as long as a month after the others.

Spring is a time of turbulent, unsettled weather when rain, sleet, wet snow, and generally socked-in conditions prevail.

Summer really begins in July and extends through September. This is when the parks are in their glory, when meadows clog with wildflowers and the temperature of Lake McDonald actually rises into the swimmable range.

Autumn is a time of clear skies and aching beauty. The grasses turn golden brown. Thickets of shrubs take on a rusty hue, and the aspens, cottonwoods, and larches change to a brilliant yellow. Deer, elk, and bighorn sheep begin to come down from their summer ranges and gather for the autumn mating season.

Snow can fall at high elevations in early September and usually sweeps through during October. But the big storms that shut down the parks and send the bears into their dens for the winter don't usually strike until November.

Lodging: Accommodations are available in both parks and in surrounding communities—particularly in East Glacier, West Glacier, St. Mary, and Waterton Townsite. In addition to the usual assortment of hotels and motels, four grand mountain lodges operate in or on the edge of the parks. These are: the Glacier Park Lodge, in East Glacier; the Many Glacier Hotel, on the shore of Swiftcurrent Lake; the Prince of Wales Hotel, overlooking Upper Waterton Lake; and Lake McDonald Lodge.

Summer is a busy season and lodging is often booked solid. Advance lodge reservations should be made. Contact Glacier Park, Inc., P.O. Box 2025, Columbia Falls, MT 59912 (tel 406-892-2525) or *www.glacierparkinc.com.*

The staff of Sun Point Chalets, once located on the shore of St. Mary Lake, awaits another busy season, circa 1920.

For information about the Waterton area, contact the Waterton Chamber of Commerce, P.O. Box 55, Waterton Park, Alberta, TOK 2MO (tel 403-859-2203), *www.watertonchamber.com.*

Backcountry Chalets: Remote Sperry and Granite Park chalets are remnants of a great chain of mountain chalets built by the Great Northern Railway for its horse-packing guests. Currently Sperry is a full service lodge, and Granite Park serves as a hikers' shelter. For information and reservations for Sperry Chalet call 888-345-2649. For Granite Park, call 406-387-5555.

Camping: Campgrounds in both parks provide basic services: tent pads, picnic tables, toilets, drinking water, and trash collection. Waterton adds cooking shelters with wood-burning stoves, stacked firewood, hot showers and, at some sites, utility hookups.

Fees vary. A night in one of Glacier's 13 camp-grounds costs $12 to $17, depending on facilities and services. At the Waterton Townsite Campground, sites with utility hookups are $23 (Canadian), those without $17. At Waterton's Crandell Mountain Campground, sites are $13. At Belly River (pit toilets) sites are $10. Campgrounds, especially in Glacier, are jammed most of the summer. Those who begin a search for a site in late afternoon are often out of luck. Reservations can be made for two campgrounds, St. Mary and Fish Creek, by calling 800-365-2267 or by visiting *http://reservations.nps.gov/.*

To avoid nasty encounters with bears, both parks require campers to take special care with food and cooking equipment. Basically, campers must keep food containers and cooking equipment in their vehicles or in a food locker except when preparing and eating meals. Trash must be disposed of in bear-resistant trash cans found along the roads and in campgrounds. These and other precautions are spelled out in detail in pamphlets handed out at the entry stations. Following the regulations is important for the safety of everyone in the campground.

Leave No Trace: This National Park Service program promotes and inspires responsible use of our public lands. "Leave No Trace" of your visit.

Pets: Pets must be on a leash no longer than six feet, under physical restraint, or caged while in the park. They are not permitted on any trail in Glacier, but they are allowed on trails in Waterton.

Emergencies: In Waterton, call 403-859-2636 for 24-hour emergency; 403-859-2244 for the police. In Glacier, call 406-888-7800; if no answer, dial 911.

Going-to-the-Sun Road Shuttle Service: At the height of the season, a shuttle bus runs the length of the Going-to-the-Sun Road, making stops at West Glacier, Apgar, Lake McDonald Lodge, The Loop, Logan Pass, Jackson Glacier Overlook, Rising Sun, and St. Mary. For information, pricing, and schedule, call Glacier Park, Inc., at 406-892-2525.

Glacier Natural History Association: For information about publications and activities contact GNHA, P.O. Box 428, West Glacier, MT, 59936 (tel 406-888-5756), *www.nps.gov/gnha.htm.*

On the Road

Glacier National Park

GLACIER NATIONAL PARK sits astride the Continental Divide in northwest Montana. Famous for its spectacular alpine panoramas and the shaggy white mountain goats that live among its highest crags, Glacier has attracted casual visitors since the 1890s, when the Great Northern Railway built its line along the southern perimeter of the present park. Many early visitors stepped off their trains in East Glacier or West Glacier and then toured the park by horse-back, spending the night under the stars or in the sumptuous digs of a grand mountain lodge. One can still reach the park by rail, and a few of the lodges continue to put up guests in high style. But the use of horses is more limited, and only a couple of the rustic backcountry chalets remain open. Still, the old horse trails delight hikers who set off on leisurely strolls or cross-country treks, and the park's roads wind through some of the most impressive scenery in North America.

THE MOST POPULAR drive follows the awesome Going-to-the-Sun Road, which runs between East Glacier and West Glacier and tops the Continental Divide at Logan Pass.

Although one is unlikely to see all of the park's major animals during a single drive, the road offers visitors the chance to see deer, elk, moose, bighorn sheep, mountain goats, bears, eagles, hawks, along with a wide variety of smaller animals.

It also presents a fine overview of the park's divided climate. The western valley, where the weather is milder and wetter, supports a cedar and hemlock forest that might seem more at home along the Pacific coast. On the east side, where a drier climate prevails, the spruce, fir and pine forests resemble those found throughout the northern Rockies.

Some of the most rewarding walks in the park start from the Going-to-the-Sun Road. A handful of short trails (a mile at most) over moderate terrain lead through ancient, cathedral-like forests, and to lovely waterfalls, sensuous gorges, and high alpine meadows choked with wildflowers. These highly recommended trails are marked on the maps.

ANOTHER POPULAR SPOT, the Many Glacier area lies in a glacially carved basin surrounded by peaks, dotted with chains of lakes, and running with waterfalls. The Many Glacier Hotel, one of the grand old lodges from the park's early days, does a brisk business on the shore of Swiftcurrent Lake. This area is the hub of a large trail network offering everything from an hour's stroll by the lake to week-long treks. In late summer and autumn, chances are good for spotting black bears and grizzlies feeding on berries. Here, too, visitors are likely to see bighorn sheep and mountain goats late in the season.

At Two Medicine Valley, a quiet pocket of the park north of East Glacier, visitors will find another glacial basin that's just a shade less dramatic than the Many Glacier area. Here, too, glaciers carved the surrounding peaks into interesting shapes and left behind a series of lakes and waterfalls. This is another likely spot for seeing bears, mountain goats, and bighorn sheep late in the season.

The remote North Fork Valley is easily the quietest sector of the park open to motorists. Roads leading through this west-side valley are narrow and rugged. The focus here is on the resiliency of forests in the face of fire. The roads pass through four recent burns: 1967, 1988, 2001, and 2003.

Deer, moose, elk, and bears live in the North Fork, but the real stars are the gray wolves that reestablished themselves there during the mid-1980s. Rarely seen today, wolves were numerous throughout Glacier until an early park policy of killing predators eliminated them. Today, their vital role in the park's natural balance is recognized.

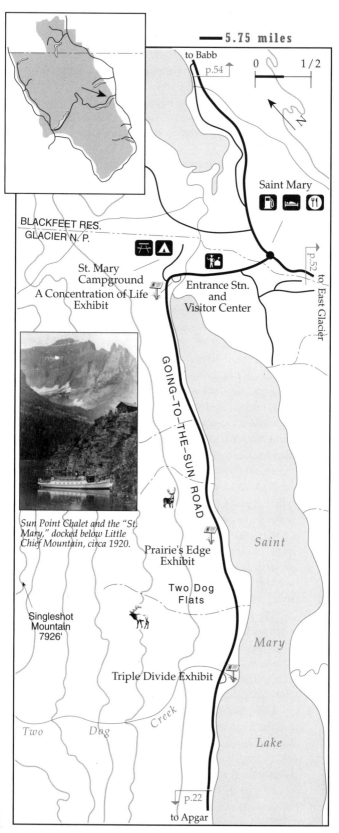

── 5.75 miles

0   1/2

N

to Babb
p.54

Saint Mary

BLACKFEET RES.
GLACIER N. P.

St. Mary
Campground
A Concentration of Life
Exhibit

Entrance Stn.
and
Visitor Center

p.52

to East Glacier

GOING-TO-THE-SUN ROAD

*Sun Point Chalet and the "St.
Mary," docked below Little
Chief Mountain, circa 1920.*

Prairie's Edge
Exhibit

Saint

Two Dog
Flats

Singleshot
Mountain
7926'

Mary

Triple Divide Exhibit

Creek

Two   Dog

Lake

p.22

to Apgar

Going-to-the-Sun Road

St. Mary: Once called Old Town, the town of St. Mary started out as a mining settlement, the center of activity for prospectors working claims at the turn of the 20th century in the St. Mary Valley.

The Lake: Ten miles long and 292 feet deep, St. Mary Lake occupies a trough gouged out by an enormous glacier thousands of years ago.

Nature Note ■ Compressed Spectrum of Habitats: As one travels north from the equator, shorter growing seasons and harsher winters determine what sorts of plants and animals inhabit the terrain. Changes in elevation influence natural surroundings in much the same way. The drive over Logan Pass compresses into 50 miles a spectrum of habitats which, at sea level, would require a north-south trip of 3,100 miles to experience. ■

Prairie Battlefield: The meadows of grasses and wildflowers that stretch down from the forests above the lake seem peaceful, but they buzz with murderous activity. Shrews paralyze grasshoppers with a special bite and cache them for later dining. Coyotes, owls, hawks, and snakes make meals of mice and meadow voles, which keep their predators well fed by knocking out several litters of young each year. Badgers break into underground burrows to gnaw on pocket gophers and ground squirrels.

In autumn, bull elk emerge from the trees at dusk to lock antlers with rivals and to bugle and bellow for mates. Their antlers weigh up to thirty pounds, and the energy expended in fighting and in mating can leave the bulls vulnerable to predators.

Singleshot Mountain: George Bird Grinnell—a pivotal force in the founding of Glacier park—dropped a bighorn on this mountain's slopes with one shot. Thus the name.

The horizontal bands of differently colored strata speak clearly of the rock's sedimentary nature. The layers that make up Glacier's mountains began forming about 1.5 billion years ago along the changing coastline of an ancient sea. Rainfall eroded slopes to the north, east, and south, and eventually deposited more than 3 to 5 miles of sand, silt, and limy mud.

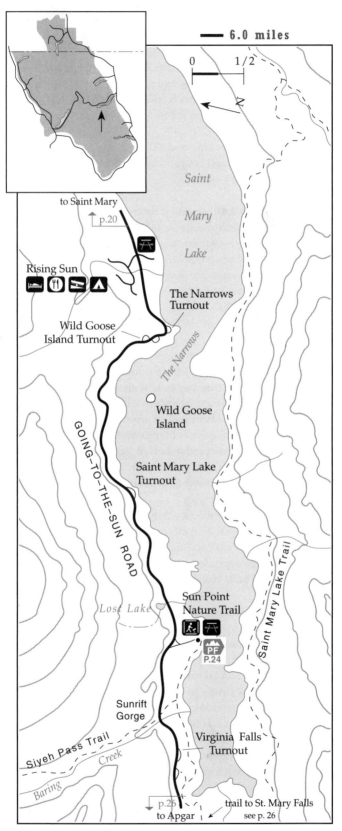

6.0 miles

0   1/2

N

to Saint Mary

p.20

Rising Sun

Saint

Mary

Lake

The Narrows Turnout

Wild Goose Island Turnout

The Narrows

Wild Goose Island

Saint Mary Lake Turnout

GOING-TO-THE-SUN ROAD

Saint Mary Lake Trail

Lose Lake

Sun Point Nature Trail

PF P.24

Sunrift Gorge

Siyeh Pass Trail

Baring Creek

Virginia Falls Turnout

p.26
to Apgar

trail to St. Mary Falls see p. 26

The Narrows: Here, two limestone points squeeze the lake to a width of just a quarter mile A footpath leads to point's end for a smashing view of the valley. About 70 million years ago, the rock that makes up the surrounding mountains lay about 40 miles west of here at the bottom of a slab of rock some 3 to 5 miles thick. As the earth's crustal plates collided to the west, this mass of rock slowly rose. Then, some time later, a huge sheet broke away from the general mass of rock and slid gradually eastward across what we now call Glacier Park. As it slid, ancient limestone at the bottom of the heap rode over rocks more than a billion years younger. The leading edge of this thrust fault block came to rest just below The Narrows.

Wild Goose Island: For good reason, this is one of the most photographed scenes in the park. Admire the view, but don't neglect the creamy limestone underfoot. Called Altyn limestone, it's part of the oldest formation on the park's east side. To get an idea how old, look up at the black ribbon of rock on the cliffs of Little Chief (see Peaks Finder, page 24). That band is roughly 750 million years old, and everything down through the Altyn layer is older, perhaps as much as 800 million years older.

St. Mary Lake Turnout: This wide turnout offers a lovely mid-lake view. The grayish-green stone in the road cut and in the guardrail is part of a mudstone formation called the Appekunny. The iron-bearing mud that made it was deposited under a primordial sea. There, the iron combined with silica to form a greenish mineral called chlorite, which colors the rock.

Virginia Falls: Across the valley, the falls drops through a gap in the trees beneath a hanging valley that was scooped out between Little Chief Mountain and Dusty Star Mountain.

    The red mudstone, decorated here with ripple marks and mud cracks that formed hundreds of millions of years ago, was made from the same iron-bearing mud that created the grayish-green Appekunny layer. However, the red stone, part of the Grinnell Formation, was deposited on tidal flats where oxygen rusted the iron components.

From Sun Point

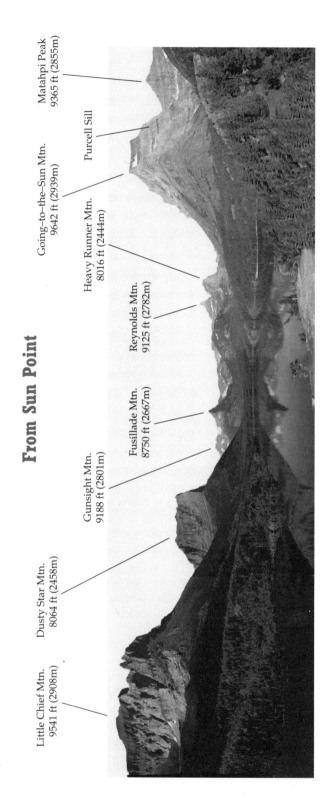

Little Chief Mtn.
9541 ft (2908m)

Dusty Star Mtn.
8064 ft (2458m)

Gunsight Mtn.
9188 ft (2801m)

Fusillade Mtn.
8750 ft (2667m)

Reynolds Mtn.
9125 ft (2782m)

Heavy Runner Mtn.
8016 ft (2444m)

Going–to–the–Sun Mtn.
9642 ft (2939m)

Purcell Sill

Matahpi Peak
9365 ft (2855m)

Reading the Landscape

■ **Glacier Tracks** ■ The rocky outcropping of Sun Point offers a tremendous view of the valley's major peaks as well as the spectacular effects of glaciation. At least three times during the past 200,000 years, huge glaciers draped the mountains, flowing down from high cirques into the valleys. The glaciers literally filled valleys like this one with rivers of slowly moving ice that gouged, rasped, plowed, and otherwise shaped the landscape as we know it today. The last of these titanic glaciers began melting away about 10,000 years ago. The park's present glaciers formed during the last several thousand years.

■ **U-Shaped Valley** ■ The tremendous force of roughly 2,000 vertical feet of moving ice studded with boulders carved out the St. Mary Valley, converting it from a narrow, V-shaped, stream-eroded canyon into this spacious, U-shaped valley. To trace the outline of the great St. Mary Valley glacier, follow the slopes between Little Chief and Going-to-the-Sun mountains.

■ **Left Hanging** ■ Hanging valleys, such as the one between Little Chief and Dusty Star, are formed when a tributary glacier flows into a much larger glacier. Because it is smaller, the tributary glacier does not gouge as deeply as the main glacier. When the two melt, the track of the tributary glacier is left hanging above that of the main glacier.

■ **Arête & Horns** ■ Arêtes are knife-edged formations carved out by glaciers working on opposite sides of a ridge. Little Chief and Dusty Star offer broadside views of arêtes. Fusillade presents a head-on view. Horns can occur when three or more glaciers gouge away at a mountain from different directions, hewing the rock into a sharp point. Reynolds Mountain offers the best example from this spot.

■ **Purcell Sill** ■ Roughly 750 million years ago, when the surrounding rock formed the bed of an ancient sea, molten magma forced its way up through the strata and moved horizontally between layers of limestone. This injected layer spread throughout what are now the park's mountains, where it can be seen as a black ribbon running across the cliffs.

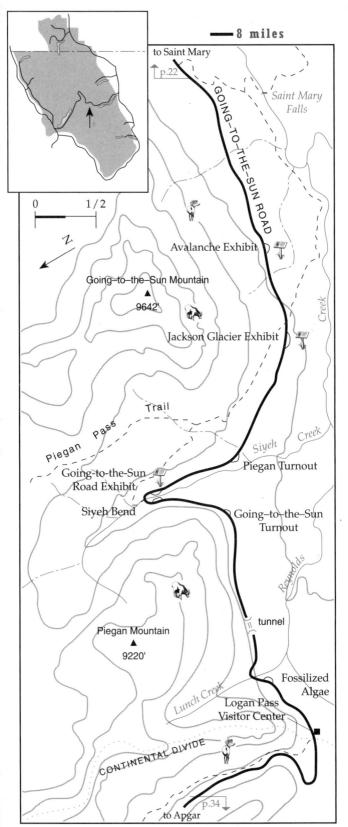

to Saint Mary

Saint Mary
Falls

p.22

GOING-TO-THE-SUN ROAD

Avalanche Exhibit

0   1/2

Going-to-the-Sun Mountain
▲
9642'

Jackson Glacier Exhibit

Creek

Trail

Piegan Pass

Siyeh Creek

Going-to-the-Sun
Road Exhibit

Piegan Turnout

Siyeh Bend

Going-to-the-Sun
Turnout

Reynolds

tunnel

Piegan Mountain
▲
9220'

Fossilized
Algae

Lunch Creek

Logan Pass
Visitor Center

CONTINENTAL DIVIDE

p.34

to Apgar

Jackson Glacier Exhibit: A sign explains how Jackson Glacier, visible over the treetops, has shrunk considerably from its mid-nineteenth-century size. The turnout overlooks a dense forest of mainly Engelmann spruce and subalpine fir, which are the dominant species on the park's drier, colder, east side.

Black bears thrive in deep forests like this, where they forage for roots, berries, buds, and grubs. Porcupines live here, too, and are not as invulnerable as their barbed quills might suggest. Fishers, large weasels rarely seen by people, feed regularly on porcupines, killing them with repeated bites to the face. Great horned owls have also been known to kill them by driving a talon through the eye into the brain.

Piegan Mountain Turnout: The mountain is named for one of the three tribes that make up the Blackfeet nation. The Piegan live on the Blackfeet Reservation east of the park.

Siyeh Bend: Here, the road makes a sharp curve and passes through a transition zone between dense forest and the scrubby subalpine vegetation typical of Glacier's high country. Mount Siyeh (elev. 10,014 feet) stands over the apex of the curve with Going-to-the-Sun Mountain on the right and Cataract and Piegan Mountains to the left. Grizzly bears roam the valley enclosed by these peaks, and mountain goats and bighorn sheep frequent the upper slopes and cliffs. Bighorn rams bash heads in the autumn for mating rights among the harems of ewes.

Nature Note ■ Fossilized Algae—Stromatolites: The dark gray, wrinkled rock at the upper end of the turnout contains the fossilized remains of algae that evolved roughly 1.5 billion years ago. This particular colony lived less than a billion years ago as mats of blue-green slime on the coast of an ancient sea. Through photosynthesis, the algae made food and added layer upon layer of a calcium carbonate crust. Called stromatolites, these laminated mounds grew into vast reefs that show up at various points in the park. They often resemble a head of cabbage cut in half. ■

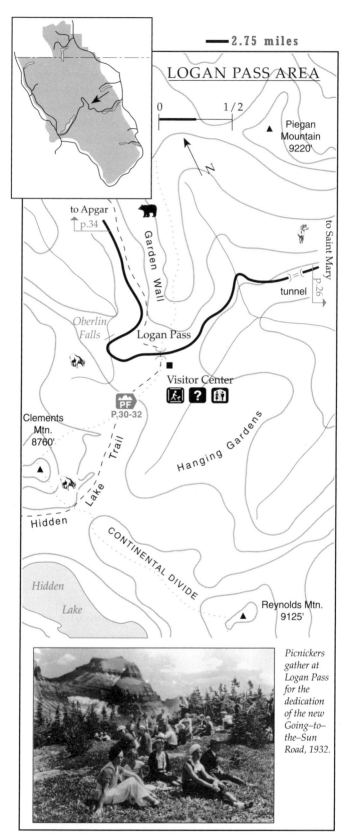

━━━━ **2.75 miles**

LOGAN PASS AREA

0 ——————— 1/2

N

Piegan
Mountain
9220'

to Apgar
p.34

Garden Wall

to Saint Mary
p.26

tunnel

Oberlin
Falls

Logan Pass

Visitor Center

PF
P.30-32

Clements
Mtn.
8760'

Hidden Lake Trail

Hanging Gardens

Hidden

CONTINENTAL DIVIDE

Hidden

Lake

Reynolds Mtn.
9125'

*Picnickers
gather at
Logan Pass
for the
dedication
of the new
Going–to–
the–Sun
Road, 1932.*

Going-to-the-Sun Road: Motorists could drive to Logan Pass as early as 1928, but the full route from St. Mary to West Glacier did not open until 1932. In some sections, workers had to slide down ropes to drill into the rock, place dynamite and blast out a ledge for the roadbed. The hard work continues today. Every spring it takes about two months to clear the road of heavy snow, which can reach a depth of 80 feet in some places.

Logan Pass: This locale is one of the most promising areas in the park to see mountain goats. Superbly adapted to leap nimbly among the highest cliffs, the creamy white goats have strong forequarters to pull them up rock faces, a heavy winter coat and two-toed hooves with spongy central pads that help grip any smooth surface. The cliffs protect them from most predators, but do not offer much grazing. As a result, goats fiercely defend food sources, jabbing at intruders with their sharp, black horns.

Hidden Lake Overlook: Above the visitor center, a boardwalk trail leads to Hidden Lake Overlook. It passes through a wide basin of rock terraces overgrown with grasses and wildflowers. Spring begins here in mid-July and night temperatures can dip below freezing anytime. The first winter snows can fall in September.

This short season, combined with the drying effects of wind and intense sunlight, have forced alpine plants to adapt in interesting ways. They can grow at temperatures close to freezing. Some, like the alpine buttercup and the glacier lily, can grow through a few inches of snow. Others sport a waxy covering to conserve moisture, or grow fuzz on leaves and stems to diffuse harsh sunshine. It is a supremely fragile environment where a new plant may take 25 years to work up enough energy to flower and reproduce. Please watch your step.

Nature Note ▪ Grizzlies: Mainly vegetarian, the park's roughly 200 grizzly bears are drawn to high meadows like those near Logan Pass in spring and summer. Here they graze on the leaves, roots, and stems of many plants and occasionally bolt down a Columbian ground squirrel or two. In fall, they grub the berry thickets along the Garden Wall to fatten up for the winter. ▪

Northeast from Logan Pass

Heavy Runner Mtn.
8016 ft (2444m)

Little Chief Mtn.
9541 ft (2908m)

Mahtotopa Peak
8881 ft (2707m)

Going-to-the-Sun Mtn.
9642 ft (2939m)

Piegan Mtn.
9220 ft (2811m)

Pollock Mtn.
9190 ft (2801m)

Garden Wall

Bishops Cap
9127 ft (2783m)

Mount Gould
9553 ft (2913m)

Reading the Landscape

■ **Formation of the Pass** ■ About a million years ago, two glaciers formed on either side of what is now Logan Pass. One scoured out St. Mary Valley; the other, McDonald Valley. They also eroded the ridge that separated them. In time, they wore away the intervening rock and merged. The ice melted several thousand years ago and exposed the pass, elevation 6,646 feet.

■ **Garden Wall** ■ Probably the park's most famous example of an arête, or knife-edged ridge, the Garden Wall stretches along the Continental Divide. This spine of rock not only separates Pacific Ocean from Hudson Bay watersheds; but it also forms a climatic divide that makes for a sharp contrast between plants in the St. Mary and McDonald Valleys.

On the McDonald side, moist air off the Pacific Ocean stalls against western slopes, where it drops most of its moisture before passing to the east side. The McDonald side is also warmer, thanks to an insulative cloud cover that traps heat. Thus, much of the McDonald Valley supports a type of forest ordinarily found in the Pacific Northwest: cedar and hemlock. The cooler, drier east side supports forests of spruce, fir, and pine that are more typical of the Northern Rockies.

■ **Going-to-the-Sun Mountain** ■ The mountain was named by George Willard Schultz and a Blackfeet friend in the 1880s while hunting. They settled on the name after noting that the peak would make a fine spot for a vision quest. Schultz later said there was no Blackfeet legend associated with the name. Even so, a story persists that the peak was named when Napi (Blackfeet creator and first-rate prankster) fled up the mountainside and disappeared into the sun.

■ **The Hoary Marmot** ■ This grizzled rodent, twice the size of a groundhog, trundles through the meadows beneath these peaks munching on roots, berries, and wildflowers. The biggest squirrel in North America, the hoary marmot spends two-thirds of its life hibernating. Marmots den under boulders and rock piles to deter hungry grizzlies. While foraging, they also risk the talons of golden eagles.

Southwest from Logan Pass

Heavy Runner Mtn.
8016 ft (2444m)

Reynolds Mtn.
9125 ft (2782m)

Hidden Lake Pass
and Overlook

Clements Mtn.
8760 ft (2671m)

Mount Oberlin
8180 ft (2494m)

Reading the Landscape

■ Remnants of a Cirque ■ The wide, flower-filled bowl above the visitor center may have once formed the floor of a cirque. The semi-circular wall of rock is thought to have extended from Heavy Runner and Reynolds Mountains to Clements Mountain. Glaciers and other erosive forces probably broke down most of the wall.

■ Hidden Lake Trail ■ This 1.5-mile, mostly board-walk, trail begins at the visitor center and leads through alpine meadows to Hidden Lake Overlook. Hikers often see mountain goats. The surfaces of some rocks along the trail bear fine examples of mud cracks and ripple marks. These patterns formed long ago, while the rock was still mud. The cracks formed as the mud dried and split apart on tidal flats. The ripple marks formed beneath waves. Some people have found marks left by raindrops that fell hundreds of millions of years ago.

■ Reynolds Mountain ■ The peak was named for Charles R. Reynolds, an editor of *Field and Stream* magazine. The Blackfeet name translates to Little Water Whiteman, which is what the tribe called Kenneth McKenzie, the most successful and ruthless leader of the American Fur Company. Upon hearing that all the horses and none of the men had been lost during a raid on one of his trapping outfits, he said, "Damn the men. If the horses had been saved it would have amounted to something."

■ Clements Mountain ■ This horn bears the name of Walter Clements, who helped negotiate the treaty that allowed the U.S. to buy the eastern half of the park from the Blackfeet. Here again, the Blackfeet name honors a more interesting character: Alexander Cul-bertson, or Beaver Child. A fur trader, Culbertson built commercially strategic Fort Benton in 1850, married into the Blackfeet tribe, and made and lost a fortune.

■ Columbian Ground Squirrels ■ Familiar characters in the Logan Pass area, the squirrels dive after grass-hoppers, pull down wildflower stems to eat the petals, and often stand on their hind feet. While hibernating, they drop their body temperatures to 37°F, reduce pulse rates to five beats a minute and breathe just once every five minutes.

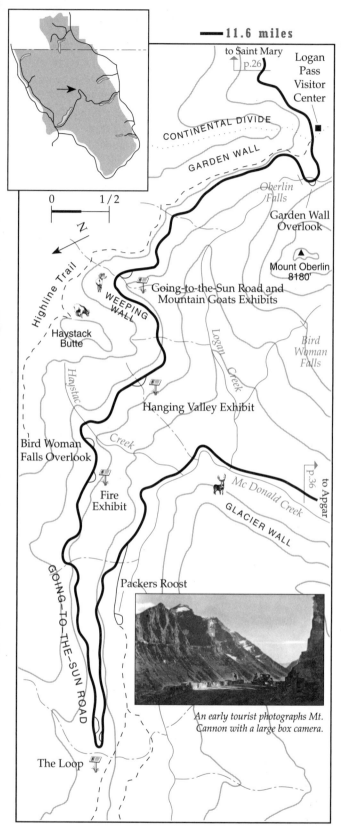

11.6 miles

to Saint Mary
p.26

Logan Pass Visitor Center

CONTINENTAL DIVIDE

GARDEN WALL

Oberlin Falls

Garden Wall Overlook

Mount Oberlin
8180'

Going-to-the-Sun Road and
Mountain Goats Exhibits

WEEPING WALL

Logan Creek

Bird Woman Falls

Highline Trail

Haystack Butte

Haystac

Hanging Valley Exhibit

Creek

Bird Woman Falls Overlook

Fire Exhibit

Mc Donald Creek

p.36

to Apgar

GLACIER WALL

GOING-TO-THE-SUN ROAD

Packers Roost

An early tourist photographs Mt. Cannon with a large box camera.

The Loop

0   1/2

N

Garden Wall Overlook: Just west of Logan Pass, a short path leads to a metal platform offering one of the park's most spectacular vistas of the Garden Wall, as well as the Lewis (right) and Livingston (left) mountain ranges. The flat-topped knob under the Garden Wall is Haystack Butte. Look for mountain goats nearby.

A thicket of dwarfed subalpine fir have grown in this relatively protected spot. The firs rarely grow much more than 15 feet high, yet some outrank by a hundred years or more the robust specimens that grow 40 to 100 feet in more forgiving climates.

Goat Slopes and Going-to-the-Sun Road: Exhibits here offer information about mountain goats and the building of the Going-to-the-Sun Road. This is an excellent place to scan the cliffs for mountain goats, the scree slopes for bighorn sheep, and the meadows for bear.

The flanks of the Garden Wall and Haystack Butte are covered with huckleberry, elderberry, and thimbleberry bushes. Every autumn, dozens of bears and thousands of birds and rodents depend on the ripe fruit for high-energy food.

Bird Woman Falls: Bird Woman Falls is the white ribbon that drops from the classic hanging valley enclosed by mounts Oberlin, Clements, and Cannon.

This turnout also presents a great view of the McDonald Valley. The U-shaped outline of the giant glacier that carved the valley can be seen along the slopes of Mount Cannon and Heaven's Peak.

From the Fire Exhibit to The Loop: The road passes through two generations of fire scars. The first area burned in 1967 and extends down the Garden Wall and across the valley to the slopes of the Glacier Wall. At The Loop, the road dips into the eastern margin of the 2003 Trapper Creek Fire. Here, entire hillsides of lodgepole pine, subalpine fir, and spruce were blackened and killed by the flames. Below, the fire spotted along McDonald Creek and into the slopes across the valley. The fire began with a lightning strike on July 21, burned into the autumn, and eventually scorched more than 19,000 acres of the upper McDonald Creek and Mineral Creek drainages. It was one of several major fires to strike the west side of the park in 2003.

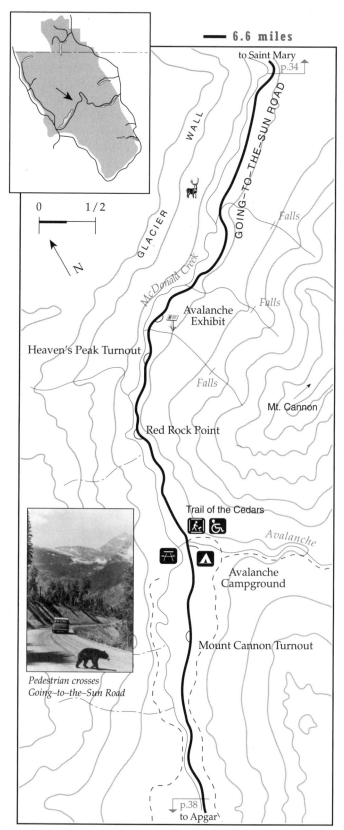

to Saint Mary p.34

GLACIER WALL

GOING-TO-THE-SUN ROAD

McDonald Creek

Falls

Avalanche Exhibit

Heaven's Peak Turnout

Falls

Mt. Cannon

Falls

Red Rock Point

Trail of the Cedars

Avalanche

Avalanche Campground

Mount Cannon Turnout

*Pedestrian crosses
Going-to-the-Sun Road*

p.38
to Apgar

Avalanche Exhibit: The awesome cascades of snow and ice that barrel down chutes like these on Mount Cannon can rip trees out by the roots or snap their trunks like matchsticks. Only more pliant types of vegetation survive in such paths. Alder, maple, willow, mountain ash, and various types of berry bushes lie bent and crushed under the heavy snow until it melts. Then these flexible shrubs bounce back.

Heaven's Peak Turnout: Here, superb views open up of Heaven's Peak (elev. 8987 feet) across McDonald Creek, and of the Garden Wall up the valley. The peak's snow and ice fields feed a network of waterfalls above the creek.

Red Rock Point: Unmarked but worth a bit of a hunt, this is perhaps the most beautiful watercourse along the park's roads. Paths lead through cedar and hemlock to McDonald Creek, which zigzags between tilting blocks of vivid red mudstone. The water gets its turquoise color from rock powder, called glacial flour. Milled by upstream glaciers, the powder remains in suspension and refracts blue light from the sky into this lovely shade of bluish green.

Down the valley, Mount Brown rises above the trees. A ridge connects it to the sharp peak of the Little Matterhorn and Mount Edwards.

Trail of the Cedars: This 0.8–mile loop trail, suitable for wheelchairs and strollers, winds through an ancient climax forest of western red cedar, hemlock, and black cottonwood. It starts on the south side of the creek and meanders among the colossal trunks to the base of Avalanche Gorge, where an achingly beautiful stretch of sapphire water swirls over rock nearly blood red.

Cedars are the trees with gray bark growing in long, spiraling strips. Black cottonwoods grow a thick, deeply furrowed bark. Hemlock crowns droop, but are difficult to see among the dense canopy.

Mount Cannon Turnout: The south-facing cliffs of Mount Cannon thunder with avalanches every winter and spring, sweeping mountain goats and bighorn sheep into the aptly named Avalanche Creek Valley. Bears, especially grizzlies, dig through the melting debris in the spring to feast on the carcasses.

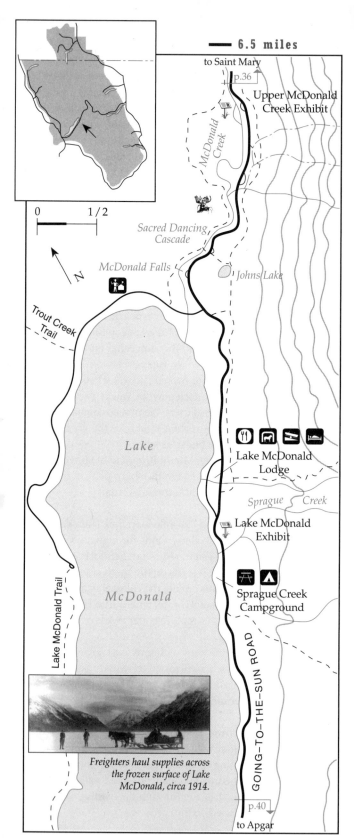

to Saint Mary

p.36

Upper McDonald
Creek Exhibit

McDonald Creek

Sacred Dancing
Cascade

McDonald Falls

Johns Lake

Trout Creek
Trail

0   1/2

N

Lake

McDonald

Lake McDonald
Lodge

Sprague   Creek

Lake McDonald
Exhibit

Sprague Creek
Campground

Lake McDonald Trail

GOING-TO-THE-SUN ROAD

*Freighters haul supplies across
the frozen surface of Lake
McDonald, circa 1914.*

p.40

to Apgar

McDonald Creek: Along the banks of McDonald Creek, white-tailed deer often appear in evening. Alert, poised, and graceful, the deer depend on concealment and an intimate knowledge of terrain to escape predators.

Nature Note ▪ Moose Country: Next to bison, moose are the largest land animals in North America. Their long legs allow them to move easily through deep snow, and their broad hooves keep them from sinking deeply into the mucky bottoms of marshy areas. During summer, moose tank up on aquatic plants rich in salt to build up a reserve that supplements their low-salt winter diet. They are at home in the water. Besides wading and dunking their heads, moose can cross lakes, swim underwater and dive as deep as fifteen feet. ▪

Sacred Dancing Cascade: A footbridge spans McDonald Creek, which splashes over the oldest rock formation on the park's west side, perhaps as old as 1.6 billion years. Dry portions of the rock may feel like good footing, but where the rock is wet, an algal slime makes the footing treacherously slick. A trail on the far bank leads upstream along Sacred Dancing Cascade, a quarter-mile series of rapids and falls. The trail downstream leads to the brink of McDonald Falls.

McDonald Falls: A stone guardrail marks the overlook for McDonald Falls, a natural barrier for native fish populations. The peaks of Stanton and Vaught stand high over the cascade.

Lake McDonald Lodge: This beautiful, rustic lodge has a spectacular log lobby with an immense stone hearth and—perhaps incongruously for a national park—the mounted heads of game trophies pinned to the balcony railings.

Lake McDonald Exhibit/2003 Fire Effects: From this vantage point, the effects of the 2003 Robert Fire can be seen clearly along the opposite shore. In places, the fire merely spotted the forest, but along the central portion of the lake, the blaze consumed entire slopes and burned all the way from the shoreline clear up to the crest of Howe Ridge and beyond into the North Fork Valley. Caused by a campfire west of the park on July 23, the fire scorched more than 57,000 acres.

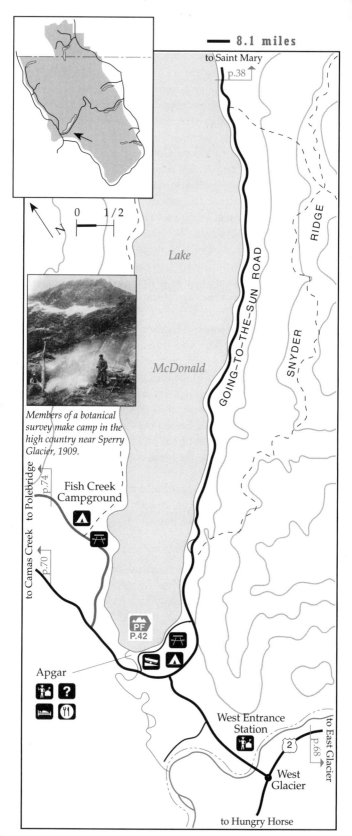

8.1 miles

to Saint Mary
p.38

Lake

McDonald

GOING-TO-THE-SUN ROAD

SNYDER RIDGE

0   1/2

N

Members of a botanical survey make camp in the high country near Sperry Glacier, 1909.

to Camas Creek
to Polebridge
p.74

p.70

Fish Creek Campground

PF
P.42

Apgar

West Entrance Station

2
p.68
to East Glacier

West Glacier

to Hungry Horse

The Forest: The road hugs Lake McDonald's east shore, but views of the water are limited because of the thick forest of hemlock, cedar, larch, white pine, and birch.

This, like most forests, can be divided into layers. At the top, the canopy of branches forms a protective roof over the forest community. Beneath the canopy grows an understory of young trees, then a shrub layer of plants that grow to about head height. Next comes the herb layer—wildflowers, grasses, and ferns. On the forest floor, mosses, mushrooms, and vines find their niches.

Nature Note ■ Animals of the Deep Forest: Other than the white-tailed deer and black bear, few large animals live in the deep forest. Still, a tremendous variety of birds, rodents, and amphibians go about their business on either side of the road. Pileated woodpeckers and great horned owls swoop between the trunks. Short-tailed weasels bound after deer mice, voles, and shrews. Bats flutter after insects. The red squirrel is probably the most familiar creature of the deep forest. Among the most intelligent of rodents, the red squirrel is bold and aggressive. It eats mostly seeds, nuts, and cones, but also scarfs down insects, bird eggs, and nestlings. ■

Pebble Beaches: Short paths lead from the many roadside turnouts to lovely pebble beaches that offer sweeping views of the mountains up the lake as well as of the effects of the 2003 Robert Fire along Howe Ridge across the water.

Lake McDonald: Lake McDonald, the largest body of water in the park, is roughly 10 miles long and 1.25-miles wide, and reaches a depth of 472 feet. On average it freezes over once every four years.

Apgar: Settlement began here in the 1890s when Milo Apgar built cabins to accommodate visitors who arrived in Belton (now West Glacier) on the Great Northern Railway.

The lodgepole pine forest between Apgar and West Glacier—fiercely defended during the 2003 Robert Fire—dates from 1929, when fire destroyed an ancient cedar and hemlock forest at this end of the park.

From Apgar

Stanton Mtn.
7750 ft (2362m)

Mount Vaught
8550 ft (2698m)

McPartland Mtn.
8413 ft (2565m)

Garden Wall

Mount Cannon
8952 ft (2729m)

Mount Brown
8565 ft (2611m)

Reynolds Mtn.
9125 ft (2782m)

Little Matterhorn
7886 ft (2402m)

Edwards Mtn.
9072 ft (2766m)

Reading the Landscape

- **Lake McDonald** ■ As with St. Mary Lake, the bed of this beautiful body of water was carved from the valley floor by an enormous glacier. The glacier formed on the Garden Wall and enlarged as others joined it from lateral valleys. The ice measured roughly 2,000 feet at its thickest. The red and green pebbles that make up the Apgar beach were carried down from colorful sedimentary formations farther up the valley.

    The lake was probably named after Duncan McDonald, a trader for the Hudson's Bay Company who camped here in 1878 and carved his name on a tree. His name was also attached to the creek, and displaced much more colorful native names, such as Sacred Dancing Waters and The Bear Wags Its Tail.

- **Howe and Snyder Ridges** ■ These ridges, which stand about 1,550 feet above the surface of the lake, are lateral moraines—great heaps of debris pushed off to either side by the great valley glacier. A heap of glacial debris also dams the lower end of the lake. The dam was formed by the McDonald Valley glacier and by gravel washed out from another glacier in the North Fork Valley.

- **The Garden Wall** ■ The wall was named during the 1890s, when George Bird Grinnell stopped at Grinnell Lake with a party of visitors. They sang a popular song of the era called Over the Garden Wall, and someone is said to have pointed to the famous arête and remarked that it was one wall you could never get over.

    That, of course, was before the Going-to-the-Sun Road was built. It traverses the Garden Wall and tops Logan Pass behind Mount Cannon. The road cannot be seen from this point.

- **Stanton Mountain** ■ This peak was named for Lottie Stanton, stalwart resident of the Kalispell area in the 1890s. Lottie and five others were visiting a local guide in 1891. When two of the party decided to climb the peak, Lottie took a more direct route and beat them to the top.

- **McPartland Mountain** ■ Frank McPartland was a copper miner who lived on Lake McDonald during the 1890s. He drowned when his boat capsized while he was crossing the lake.

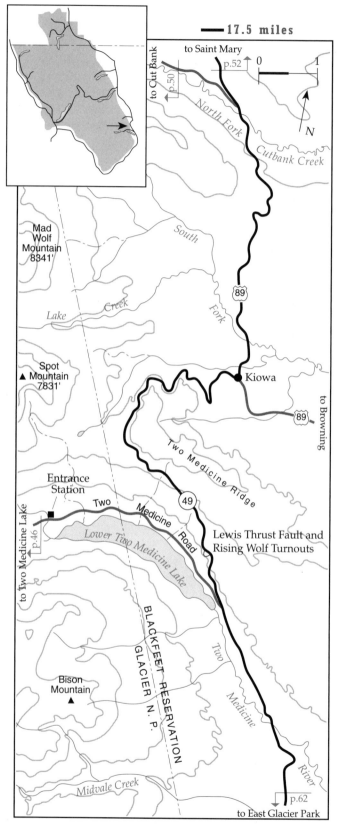

to Saint Mary

to Cut Bank

17.5 miles

p.52

0   1

N

North Fork

Cutbank Creek

South

Fork

89

Mad
Wolf
Mountain
8341'

Lake

Creek

Spot
▲ Mountain
7831'

Kiowa

89

to Browning

Two Medicine Ridge

Entrance
Station

49

Two   Medicine

Road

Lewis Thrust Fault and
Rising Wolf Turnouts

to Two Medicine Lake

p.46

Lower Two Medicine Lake

Bison
Mountain ▲

BLACKFEET   RESERVATION

GLACIER   N. P.

Two

Medicine

River

Midvale Creek

p.62

to East Glacier Park

East Glacier to Babb

The Blackfeet Reservation: East of the park, perimeter
roads lead through the Blackfeet Reservation. Long
ago, the Blackfeet migrated across the Great Plains to
the valley of the North Saskatchewan River. There,
they lived as an independent, stone-age people, hunting
the buffalo (bison) on foot and moving their posses-
sions about on the backs of dogs.

After acquiring the horse and gun in the early eigh-
teenth century, the Blackfeet expanded their territory
south to include the eastern half of what is now Glacier
Park and the rolling prairie to the east. For more than
a century, the Blackfeet were the dominant military
force, Indian or Anglo, on the northwestern plains.

Three politically independent tribes make up the
Blackfeet people: the Piegan (pronounced *PAY–gan*),
the Blood and the Northern Blackfoot.

Nature Note ■ Stunted Aspens: As the road curves
around Two Medicine Ridge, a landscape of wrinkled
grassland opens to the north. Wide groves of aspen fill
the swales. Strong winds force these trees to grow close
to the ground, while deep snow and the shade of their
neighbors cause many to grow a dense bulb of foliage
atop denuded trunks. Some have such thick trunks that
they resemble giant mushrooms. ■

Rising Wolf Mountain Turnout: Rising Wolf Mountain,
broad and angular, stands high above Lower Two
Medicine Lake. Rising Wolf is the Blackfeet name for
Hugh Monroe, a Hudson's Bay Company employee
who quit his job in 1817 to live with the tribe (see
page 47).

Lewis Thrust Fault: A major geologic feature, the Lewis
Thrust Fault runs in a diagonal line along the upper
cliffs of Bison Mountain (see photo inset, page 46).

Two Medicine River: Named for the Piegan and Blood
tradition of building two adjacent medicine lodges
for the annual Sun Dance, this river winds through
a valley of prairie and dense conifer forest. In areas
like this, the Blackfeet found deer, elk, moose, and
the means to kill them. Serviceberry and chokecherry
bushes provided wood for bows and arrows.

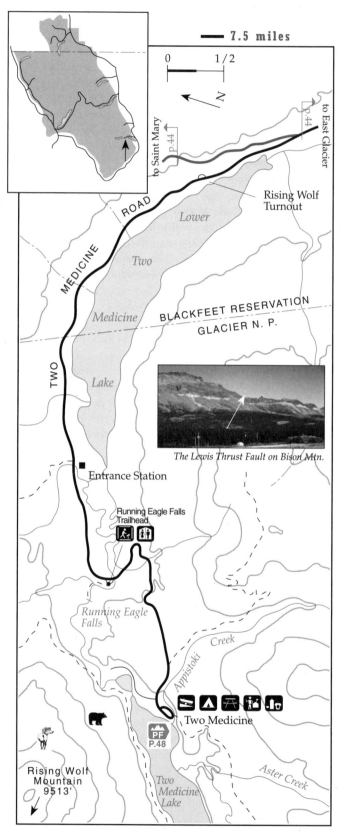

7.5 miles

0   1/2

N

to Saint Mary
p.44

to East Glacier
p.44

MEDICINE ROAD

Lower

Two

Medicine

Lake

TWO

Rising Wolf
Turnout

BLACKFEET RESERVATION

GLACIER N. P.

The Lewis Thrust Fault on Bison Mtn.

Entrance Station

Running Eagle Falls
Trailhead

*Running Eagle
Falls*

Appistoki

Creek

Two Medicine

PF
P.48

Rising Wolf
Mountain
9513'

*Two
Medicine
Lake*

Aster Creek

Two Medicine Road

Two Medicine Valley: This broad, glacially carved valley got its name from a tradition of two Blackfeet tribes, the Blood and Piegan, who often held their annual Sun Dance in adjacent medicine lodges. Still practiced, the dance is an important religious ceremony for many Plains Indian people. An act of the whole tribe, it expresses the paramount importance of the common good.

Lewis Thrust Fault: The Lewis Thrust Fault runs in a diagonal line along the face of the rounded mountain to the southwest (see map inset). The fault marks the surface on which a vast sheet of billion-year-old rock slid about 40 miles east across a layer of shale just 60 to 70 million years old.

Rising Wolf Turnout: Easily the most prominent mountain in the valley, Rising Wolf was the Blackfeet name of Hugh Monroe, an adopted member of the tribe. Monroe came west around 1817 as a Hudson's Bay Company agent assigned to spend a year with the Blackfeet and learn their language and customs. Monroe enjoyed the tribal way of life so much that he chucked the Hudson's Bay job and spent the rest of his days with the Blackfeet. He died in 1899 at age 93.

Nature Note ■ Black Bear: The mixed forest of aspen, cottonwood, and various conifers surrounding Lower Two Medicine Lake makes an excellent habitat for black bears. As predatory as these large, powerful animals may seem, Glacier's roughly 500 black bears depend on meat for just five to ten percent of their diet. If they get meat, it's likely to be carrion or small mammals such as mice and voles. Mainly they eat twigs, buds, berries, roots, and nuts. ■

Running Eagle Falls: Past the park entry station, the road heads straight for Sinopah Mountain then skirts an intervening ridge made of hard limestone roughly 1.5 billion years old. Over the ridge spills Running Eagle Falls, also known as Trick Falls because of its varying appearance from season to season as water levels change. A short path leads to the falls through a forest of massive Engelmann spruce, lodgepole, and cottonwood. The waterfall is named for a Blackfeet woman who is said to have led raids on enemy tribes.

From Two Medicine Lake

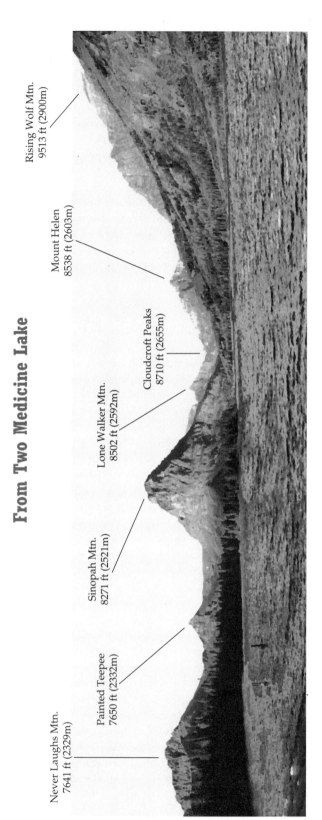

Rising Wolf Mtn.
9513 ft (2900m)

Mount Helen
8538 ft (2603m)

Cloudcroft Peaks
8710 ft (2655m)

Lone Walker Mtn.
8502 ft (2592m)

Sinopah Mtn.
8271 ft (2521m)

Painted Teepee
7650 ft (2332m)

Never Laughs Mtn.
7641 ft (2329m)

Reading the Landscape

■ **Two Medicine Lake** ■ As in most of the deep mountain lakes in Glacier-Waterton, very little aquatic vegetation grows in Two Medicine Lake. This is partly due to a shore that drops off quickly to a maximum depth of 260 feet, making it difficult for rooted plants to establish themselves. Also, the deep, cold water retards the decomposition of organic matter, which would release nutrients to fertilize aquatic vegetation. Look for mule deer along the water's edge, snowshoe hares in the campground and, in the autumn, bighorn sheep and bears on the slopes of the mountains.

■ **Sinopah Mountain** ■ Named for the Blackfeet wife of Hugh Monroe, Sinopah Mountain looks like a fat, inverted cone from this angle. Actually, it is the prow of a knife-edged ridge that leads straight back for about 2 miles. Though not as sharp as some other arêtes, Sinopah was formed the same way, by glacial gouging from both sides.

■ **Lone Walker Mountain** ■ Another peak in the Monroe family album, Lone Walker takes its name from Hugh's father-in-law. Lone Walker kept 16 wives in five tepees and is said to have had friends among the Mandan, clear over in present North Dakota. He also had a pair of pet bears that followed him around camp and lolled in front of his tepee. This scared Monroe initially, but he got over his jitters when Lone Walker spat into Hugh's hands and rubbed them on the bears.

■ **Painted Teepee** ■ An arête in miniature, the peak from this perspective is clearly reminiscent of the lodges made by native families from cured buffalo skins and lodgepole pines. Sturdy, weatherproof, and portable, the tepee made a fine shelter for their nomadic life.

Painted tepees were special because they offered more than physical shelter. They were works of religious art. The Blackfeet painted murals on the outsides of their lodges that portrayed creatures that the lodge owner regarded as the source of his spiritual power. These silhouettes of buffalo, elk, and beaver, for example, were painted in strict obedience to instructions received in a vision. At the bottom of the tepee, red bands symbolized the earth. At the top, a blackened area represented the night sky, often with unpainted circles for stars.

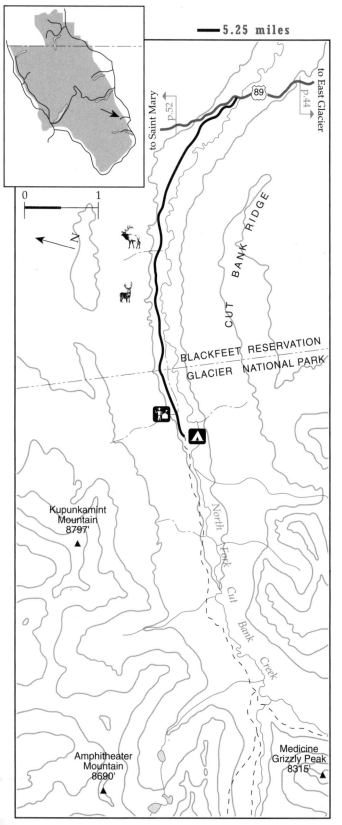

to Saint Mary
p.52

89

to East Glacier
p.44

CUT BANK RIDGE

BLACKFEET RESERVATION

GLACIER NATIONAL PARK

0   1

N

Kupunkamint
Mountain
8797'
▲

North Fork Cut Bank Creek

Amphitheater
Mountain
8690'
▲

Medicine
Grizzly Peak
8315' ▲

Cut Bank Road

Cut Bank Valley Road: This gravel road leads for 5 miles along Cut Bank Creek to a ranger station and campground set among stands of mature lodgepole, Engelmann spruce, and fir. Broad meadows of prairie grasses and wildflowers stretch over the south-facing slopes, opening up fine views of the mountains surrounding Cut Bank Pass at the head of the valley. At dusk, deer and elk often walk the fringes of the meadows.

Prairie Meadows: Here among the prairie meadows of the Cut Bank Valley, shrews, whose hearts beat a thousand times a minute, are hard at work. They eat almost anything they manage to kill: insects, spiders, even mice and—along the creek in the forest—slugs, salamanders, spiders, small fish, and tadpoles. They see poorly, but they have a good sense of smell and some types even use echolocation to find prey.

As the world's smallest mammals, shrews face an interesting challenge. Because of their high surface area relative to body mass, they lose body heat very quickly. To compensate, they must maintain an astonishing metabolic rate—and that takes lots of food. If they do not eat several times their body weight each day, they die.

Nature Note ■ Mountain Lions: Although park visitors are very unlikely to see a mountain lion, these cats, which can weigh more than 200 pounds, stalk deer and elk in areas like the Cut Bank Valley. Also called cougars and pumas, mountain lions often hunt by crouching for hours in branches that overhang game trails. They drop onto the backs of passing deer, elk, and moose, and kill by sliding their teeth between the vertebrae and cutting the spinal cord. It's a dangerous way to make a living. A full-grown elk can weigh three times (and a moose nearly ten times) as much as a big lion. If the killing bite is not swift, the lion risks being gored, kicked, or slammed against trees. It's not unusual for them to die trying to take down a big animal. When they can't get big game, lions hunt smaller mammals, including porcupines. Killing porcupines is a delicate task, apparently requiring a deft paw to flip and stun the animal before biting the underside. Young lions have died from porcupine-quill wounds. ■

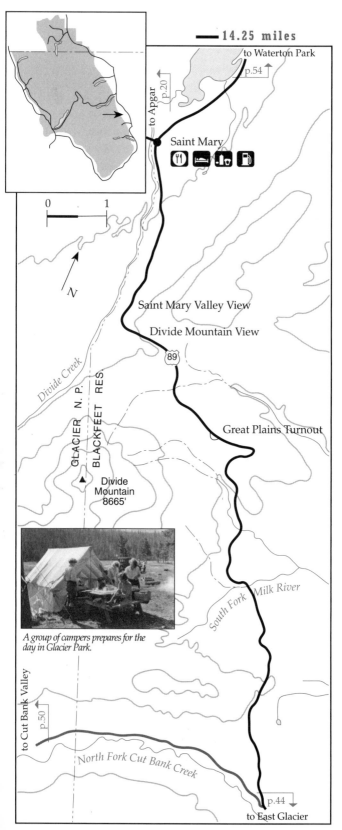

— **14.25 miles**

to Waterton Park

4

to Apgar

p.20

Saint Mary

0 1

N

Saint Mary Valley View

Divide Mountain View

89

Divide Creek

GLACIER N. P.

BLACKFEET RES.

Great Plains Turnout

▲ Divide Mountain 8665'

South Fork Milk River

A group of campers prepares for the day in Glacier Park.

to Cut Bank Valley

p.50

North Fork Cut Bank Creek

p.44

to East Glacier

2

St. Mary Valley: Along US 89 south of St. Mary, good vistas open up of the St. Mary Valley to the west. Note the broad, U-shape of the glacially carved valley.

Divide Mountain View: A grand arch of gray stone that bursts from the surrounding spruce-fir forest, Divide Mountain (elev. 8665 feet) sits astride the Hudson Bay Divide. Snow melt from this side of the peak eventually trickles northeast to Hudson Bay. Water from the other side runs down the Mississippi River into the Gulf of Mexico.

Great Plains Turnout: Until the mid-1870s, the plains visible from this high vantage point supported immense herds of bison, the driving force of the Blackfeet economy. Buffalo provided not only food, but also the materials for making bags, packs, tepee covers, belts, robes, mittens, caps, moccasins, rope, halters, watering troughs, and rattles. Horns made powder flasks. Sinew threaded garments and strung bows. Rib bones made good sled runners. Boiled bull phalluses provided glue, and dung burned well as fuel.

    The Blackfeet ate other game only when they couldn't get buffalo, which they called "real food." They hunted the animal all year: bulls in early summer, cows in fall, calves in spring. During winter, when the shaggy hair was longest, they killed for the robes they traded with the Anglos.

South Fork Milk River: For some distance north of the bridge, the road passes through a boggy flat thick with shrubs. This is prime habitat for beaver. White traders encouraged the Blackfeet to gather beaver pelts, which fetched a high price in the early nineteenth century. Although a single Blackfeet could have harvested about a hundred beaver a month using a bow and arrows, most members of the tribe had an aversion to killing beaver, a sacred animal.

Cut Bank Valley: This broad, grassy valley (see map p. 50) leads to Cut Bank Pass, a popular route through the mountains for generations of natives. The Blackfeet guarded it to discourage western tribes from hunting buffalo. In 1866, a large force of Gros Ventre and Crow warriors attacked the Piegan tribe northwest of here, but the Piegan routed them.

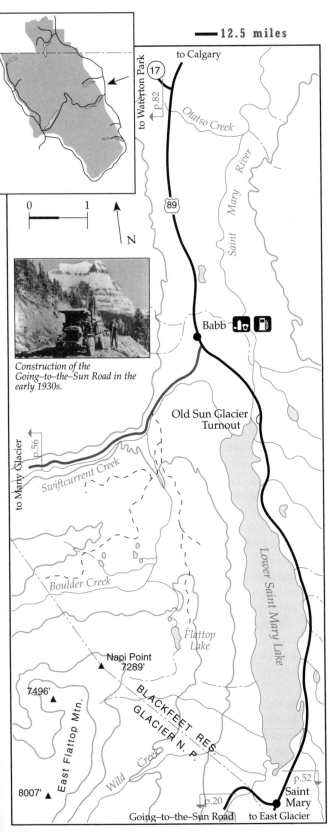

━━━ 12.5 miles

to Calgary

to Waterton Park p.82

(17)

Otatso Creek

89

Saint Mary River

Babb

Old Sun Glacier
Turnout

*Construction of the
Going-to-the-Sun Road in the
early 1930s.*

0   1

N

to Many Glacier p.56

Swiftcurrent Creek

Lower Saint Mary Lake

Boulder Creek

Flattop
Lake

Napi Point
7289'

7496'

BLACKFEET RES.

GLACIER N. P.

Wild Creek

East Flattop Mtn.

8007'

p.20

p.52

Saint
Mary

Going-to-the-Sun Road   to East Glacier

Babb: The roots of this tiny community can be traced back to 1874, when a trader named John Kennedy set up a trading post nearby. The isolated, conical peak that keeps appearing over the ridge to the northwest is Chief Mountain, a sacred site among the Blackfeet.

Old Sun Glacier: From here, almost due west, the gleaming summit of Merritt Peak (elev. 10,004 feet) pokes over the crests of the nearest mountains. The white sheet draped across Merritt is Old Sun Glacier, one of the few glaciers visible from the roads. Like all of the park's glaciers, Old Sun formed within the last several thousand years and had virtually nothing to do with the heavy glaciation that carved out the park's mountains.

Napi Point: Across the lake, a zigzagging line divides a mixed forest of evergreens and aspens from a silvery gray blanket of dead trees killed during a 1984 fire. Called the Napi Point Fire, it burned 3,400 acres of forest and passed over the facing ridge into the next valley. The fire scar runs all along the northern end of Lower Saint Mary Lake. Touched off by lightning, the fire burned itself out in 15 days. The fire line leads to the abrupt cliff, called Napi Point, at the end of East Flattop Mountain.

Napi Rock: The cone-shaped pinnacle at the northern end of Singleshot Mountain is named after Napi, the central character in Blackfeet cosmology. Napi, or Old Man, created the world and every living thing in it. He and his wife, Old Woman, designed people and built death into their creation so people would feel sorry for one another. Napi also taught the first people to collect edible plants, make weapons, hunt animals, and fashion clothing. There are many stories about Napi's adventures among the early Blackfeet, some quite earthy.

Nature Note ■ Fire Effects: The results of a 2002 fire can be seen along the ridge northeast of the town of St. Mary. Though it destroys, fire also creates. It admits sunlight to the forest floor, where new plants grow quickly in soil enriched by ash. The plants feed elk, moose, deer, bears, and a host of smaller mammals. ■

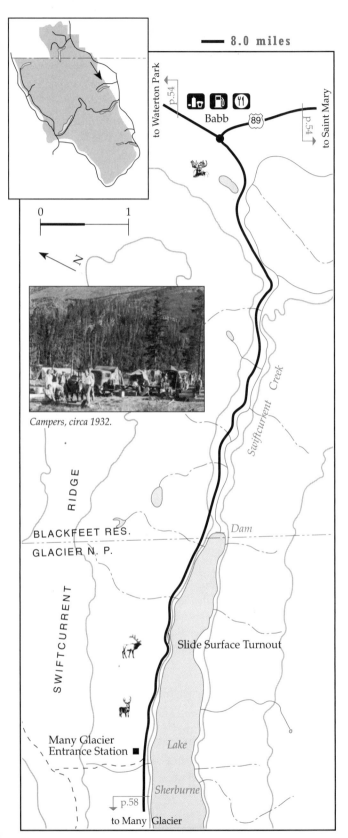

8.0 miles

to Waterton Park

p.54

Babb

89

to Saint Mary

p.54

0   1

N

Campers, circa 1932.

Swiftcurrent Creek

R I D G E

Dam

BLACKFEET RES.

GLACIER N. P.

S W I F T C U R R E N T

Slide Surface Turnout

Lake

Many Glacier
Entrance Station

Sherburne

p.58

to Many Glacier

Many Glacier Area

East Flattop Mountain: In 1987, a fire raced over the slopes of East Flattop Mountain (across the valley on the left), opening new terrain for many types of wildflowers, grasses, and shrubs. In a sense, modern forest fires recreate a key event in the evolution of humans. Some 100 million years ago, the planet's climate changed from tropical to temperate. Vast coniferous forests burned or died off. In their place, a new class of plants evolved—flowering plants that enclosed their seeds in highly nutritive casings. These seeds provided high-energy food for the warm blooded, rat-like creatures that humans evolved from.

Swiftcurrent Creek: The road follows Swiftcurrent Creek and skirts a thick forest of lodgepole, spruce, and fir. In forests like this, red squirrels gather pine nuts, chatter irritably at intruders, and scurry for their lives from pine martens. About the size of a cat, the pine marten is a type of weasel, brown with pale ears and a long, bushy tail. Its semi-retractable claws allow it to match the agility of squirrels in deadly, treetop scrambles.

Prairie Meadows: Here and there, the trees give way to broad meadows of prairie grasses and shrubs as well as some marshy areas. This is fine habitat for members of the deer family—elk, moose, and both mule and white-tailed deer. Males grow a new set of antlers annually, a process that takes a physical toll greater than that incurred by females during pregnancy and lactation.

Lake Sherburne: Originally two lakes, Sherburne became one after construction of the dam in 1916 raised the water level. The initial lake beds were scooped out by a huge glacier that coalesced in the Many Glacier Valley and plowed its way down to the plains near Babb.

Wynn Mountain: Glacier's mountains once lay at the base of a vast sheet of rock three to five miles thick, 20 wide and about a hundred long. The sheet slid about 40 miles east and came to rest here. Wynn Mountain, across the valley, lies along the leading edge of the sheet, which moved across a lubricating layer of clay. The clay, now dark shale, can be seen along the shore beneath this turnout.

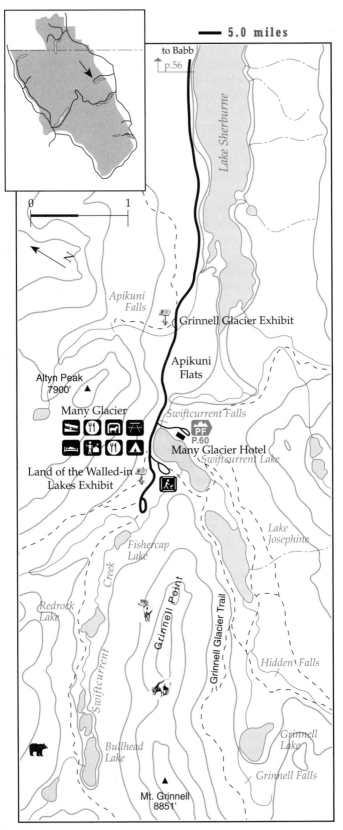

to Babb
↑ p.56

Lake Sherburne

0   1

N

Apikuni
Falls

Grinnell Glacier Exhibit

Apikuni
Flats

Altyn Peak
7900'

Swiftcurrent Falls

Many Glacier

PF
P.60

Many Glacier Hotel

Land of the Walled-in
Lakes Exhibit

Swiftcurrent Lake

Fishercap
Lake

Lake
Josephine

Redrock
Lake

Grinnell Point

Grinnell Glacier Trail

Swiftcurrent

Creek

Hidden Falls

Bullhead
Lake

Grinnell
Lake

Grinnell Falls

Mt. Grinnell
8851'

Grinnell Glacier: Just beyond the park entry station, the road heads straight toward a portion of the Garden Wall that includes Grinnell Glacier and Grinnell Falls. Much diminished, the glacier once covered most of the wall visible from here and connected with the large, upper strip of white called The Salamander.

Apikuni Falls: To the right, the slopes of Apikuni and Altyn peaks droop to form the lip of a small hanging valley. Apikuni Creek runs over the lip forming a waterfall. A trail leads to the falls from the Grinnell Glacier Exhibit. Here, the sedimentary nature of the rock shows clearly in the cliffs. The layers collected along the shifting coast of an ancient sea more than one billion years ago.

Altyn: In 1898, the eastern half of today's park was thrown open to seekers of gold, copper, oil, and natural gas. On Apikuni Flats south of the road, miners and roughnecks built the town of Altyn—a boomtown temporary home of some 200 souls. They dug mine shafts, dragged a 16,000-pound ore concentrator up Cracker Canyon and drilled wells. Luckily, none of what they sought existed in sufficient quantity to prevent the formation of Glacier National Park in 1910.

Years ago, the flats were the customary lambing grounds for mountain sheep, which still gather there during late autumn.

Swiftcurrent Falls: A short trail runs along the edge of the falls, which drops over limestone formed more than a billion years ago and runs out over a layer of rock just 60 to 70 million years old. This is a likely spot to see a water ouzel, or dipper. These small, gray birds plunge beneath the rushing water and walk along the streambed looking for insects.

Many Glacier Hotel: The Great Northern Railway built this sprawling, Swiss-style lodge in 1914–15 from native stone and massive logs. Task completed, the railroad stalled the dismantling of a nearby sawmill until 1925, when the head of the park service lost patience. He had crews place dynamite charges, then invited hotel guests to step outside and watch him blow it up.

From Many Glacier

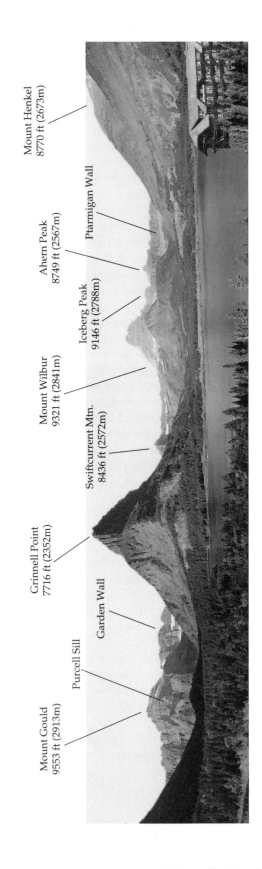

Mount Gould
9553 ft (2913m)

Purcell Sill

Garden Wall

Grinnell Point
7716 ft (2352m)

Swiftcurrent Mtn.
8436 ft (2572m)

Mount Wilbur
9321 ft (2841m)

Iceberg Peak
9146 ft (2788m)

Ahern Peak
8749 ft (2567m)

Ptarmigan Wall

Mount Henkel
8770 ft (2673m)

60

Reading the Landscape

■ **Rivers of Ice** ■ All of the valleys leading into Swift-current Lake bear the unmistakable, U-shaped tracks of the glaciers that filled this panorama with moving ice thousands of years ago. The ice oozed down on either side of Mount Gould and scraped past Grinnell Point, where it joined other glaciers that had formed on both sides of Mount Wilbur and along the Ptarmigan Wall. These ice sheets combined into one massive glacier that flowed on down the valley and out to the plains.

■ **Purcell Sill** ■ This black band of volcanic rock sandwiched between thin layers of light-colored limestone runs across the cliffs of Mount Gould, the Garden Wall, Mount Wilbur, and portions of the Ptarmigan Wall. About 750 million years old, the Purcell Sill formed when molten magma rose from beneath the Earth's crust and spread horizontally between layers of rock that lay below an ancient sea.

■ **Mount Gould** ■ Going-to-the-Sun Road traverses the back side of Mount Gould and the Garden Wall. As cars climb past the left side of the mountain, they travel at an elevation roughly 1,125 feet higher than the surface of Swiftcurrent Lake.

■ **Grinnell Point** ■ Named for the great advocate of conservation, George Bird Grinnell, this monumental prow of rock extends back three miles to Mount Grinnell (elev. 8851 feet), which cannot be seen from this angle.

■ **Major Mammals** ■ This area is one of the park's best roadside settings for spotting mountain goats, bighorn sheep, and bears. Goats frequent the upper cliffs of Grinnell Point. Sheep appear in late summer and fall among the high meadows and scree slopes of Grinnell Point, Altyn Peak, and Mount Henkel.

Every autumn, grizzlies and black bears paw through the shrubs for berries on the lower slopes of Grinnell Point, Altyn, and Henkel. The berry feast not only fuels them for the winter. It can also decide whether sows have cubs. A sow may mate in the summer, but her embryo may not attach to the uterine wall until late summer or autumn—and then only if she has put on enough fat to carry her and her cubs through the winter.

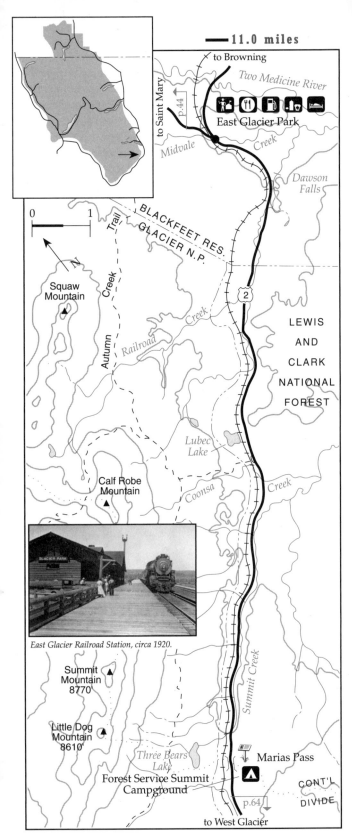

to Browning

Two Medicine River

East Glacier Park

to Saint Mary

p.44

Midvale

Creek

Dawson Falls

BLACKFEET RES.
GLACIER N.P.

Trail

2

Squaw
Mountain

Creek

Autumn

Railroad

Creek

LEWIS
AND
CLARK
NATIONAL
FOREST

Lubec Lake

Calf Robe
Mountain

Coonsa

Creek

East Glacier Railroad Station, circa 1920.

Summit
Mountain
8770'

Little Dog
Mountain
8610'

Summit Creek

Three Bears Lake

Marias Pass

Forest Service Summit
Campground

CONT'L

DIVIDE

p.64

to West Glacier

0   1

N

East Glacier: Known as Midvale before the park's founding in 1910, this community got its start as a depot town for the Great Northern Railway, which built its line from St. Paul to Seattle in the early 1890s. When talk stirred of establishing a national park here, the railroad saw a chance to boost passenger and freight traffic along its 60-mile stretch of track between East Glacier and West Glacier. The Great Northern threw its political weight behind creation of the park and then played a key role in the development of Glacier during the early years.

Perhaps the railroad's most notable legacy is the network of grand lodges and chalets it built throughout the park for wealthy visitors who arrived by train to see the mountains on horseback. Only a handful of the buildings remain, including the impressive Glacier Park Hotel here in town. The hotel was built in 1912–13 on a frame of unpeeled logs cut from cedar and Douglas fir trees 500 to 800 years old. The hotel is open to anyone during the season.

Marias Pass: For most of the drive between East Glacier and Marias Pass, the road runs over terrain characteristic of the park's eastern fringe. Grassy hills mix with groves of aspen and bands of dark evergreens. Streambeds grow thick with willows and other shrubs.

Western Peaks: The peaks to the west owe their colorful flanks to a sedimentation process that took place along the shifting coast of a primeval ocean more than one billion years ago. Both red and grayish-green layers are made of the same iron-bearing mudstone, argillite. However, the red stone was deposited on tidal flats, where it oxidized, or rusted, in the open air. The grayish-green was deposited in deep water.

Nature Note ■ Coyotes: The mixed forest and grassland habitat makes a rich hunting ground for coyotes, a highly intelligent animal roughly the size of a German shepherd. Coyotes eat ground squirrels, rabbits, mice, and voles and have been known to bob in streams for crayfish and suckers. When a badger digs for ground squirrels, a coyote often waits nearby, staking out the burrow's scoot holes, ready to pounce when the squirrels make a run for it. ■

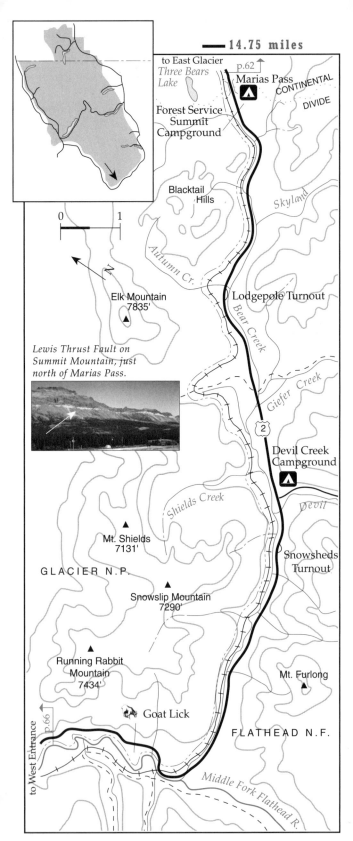

━━ **14.75 miles**

to East Glacier
Three Bears Lake
p.62
Marias Pass
CONTINENTAL
DIVIDE

Forest Service
Summit
Campground

Blacktail
Hills

Skyland

Autumn Cr.

0   1

N

Elk Mountain
7835'

Lodgepole Turnout

Bear Creek

Giefer Creek

*Lewis Thrust Fault on
Summit Mountain, just
north of Marias Pass.*

2

Devil Creek
Campground

Devil

Shields Creek

Mt. Shields
7131'

Snowsheds
Turnout

GLACIER N.P.

Snowslip Mountain
7290'

Running Rabbit
Mountain
7434'

Mt. Furlong

p.66
Goat Lick

FLATHEAD N.F.

to West Entrance

Middle Fork Flathead R.

Marias Pass: Pronounced *muh–RYE–us*, this strategic pass once provided access to the buffalo hunting grounds of the Great Plains for west-side tribes such as the Kootenai and Salish. However, the east-side Blackfeet later shut down the pass by ambushing hunting parties that ventured forth.

Signs at the rest area here summarize the significance of the pass to railroad and highway builders, and a monument commemorates President Theodore Roosevelt's interest in conservation. On the peaks across the highway, one can trace the line of the Lewis Thrust Fault (see photo map inset), a major geologic feature.

Nature Note ■ Lodgepole Pine: Here, a mature stand of lodgepole pine sways high above the road. When lodgepoles sprout close together, they grow straight and slender, shedding lower branches as the forest canopy shades their trunks. Younger specimens made fine poles for the lodges of Plains Indian tribes. Hence the name. Fire actually helps lodgepole pines reproduce. The heat bursts open many of their cones, allowing the seeds to be released. The seeds germinate in the ash-richened soil and grow quickly in sunny areas opened by the fire. After about 50 to 60 years, they look like the trees here. ■

Avalanche Chutes: Aptly named, Snowslip Mountain thunders with avalanches during winter and early spring. These dangerous snowslides can reach speeds of 130 mph, sweeping everything but the most limber shrubs from their paths. Avalanche chutes, like the one on the north side of the road, crisscross the slopes of Snowslip, Running Rabbit, and Shields Mountains. They account for the sheds built over the tracks.

Goat Lick: A short, asphalt path leads to a viewing stand overlooking the blue waters of the Middle Fork Flathead River. Here, the current has cut deeply into the easily eroded soil, creating steep drop-offs and exposing a mass of gray, clay-containing minerals craved by mountain goats. Usually, the goats live among the highest cliffs of Glacier's mountains and are rarely seen below timberline. During late June and July, though, dozens at a time gather here.

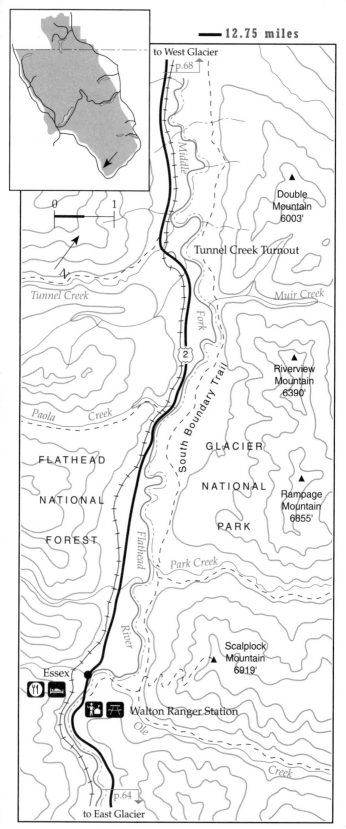

━━━ **12.75 miles**

to West Glacier
p.68

Double
Mountain
6003'

Tunnel Creek Turnout

Muir Creek

0   1

N

Tunnel Creek

Middle

Fork

2

Riverview
Mountain
6390'

Paola   Creek

FLATHEAD

South Boundary Trail

GLACIER

NATIONAL

Rampage
Mountain
6855'

NATIONAL

FOREST

Flathead

PARK

Park Creek

Scalplock
Mountain
6919'

River

Essex

Walton Ranger Station

Ole

Creek

p.64
to East Glacier

Tunnel Creek: Here, trains pass through the hillside beneath the road, cross Tunnel Creek, and then shoot into another tunnel about three-fourths of a mile up the highway.

Larch Grove: Beneath the Tunnel Creek turnout, the river makes a sharp, right-hand bend. The point of land across the river is thick with larch trees, the only conifer in Glacier that drops its needles every year. In the autumn, larch needles turn yellow, adding their splash of color to the aspens and cottonwoods that also grow along the river. The thick, reddish bark of larches helps them survive periodic fires that clear out the lodgepoles, which explains why some stand high over the rest of the forest. The trees can grow as tall as 180 feet and reach trunk diameters of 38 inches. Some individuals may be 700 years old.

Nature Note ■ Deep Forests: The thick forests that line the road reflect the wetter, warmer climate of Glacier's west side. Note the density of the forest and the lush undergrowth. At night in forests like this, flying squirrels glide from tree to tree in search of pine nuts, lichen, mushrooms, and other fungi. To glide, flying squirrels use wide flaps of skin that extend from wrist to ankle, and they help control their flight with a long, flattened, furry tail. Just before landing, they rear up and stall out. ■

Essex: Train buffs may want to stop at the Izaak Walton Inn, a lodge built by the Great Northern Railway. In years past, crews housed at the inn kept the tracks clear of snow and ran the "helper engines" that boosted trains over the steep grade.

Belton began with a few railroad cars on a sidetrack. It grew with the park and in 1949 was renamed West Glacier.

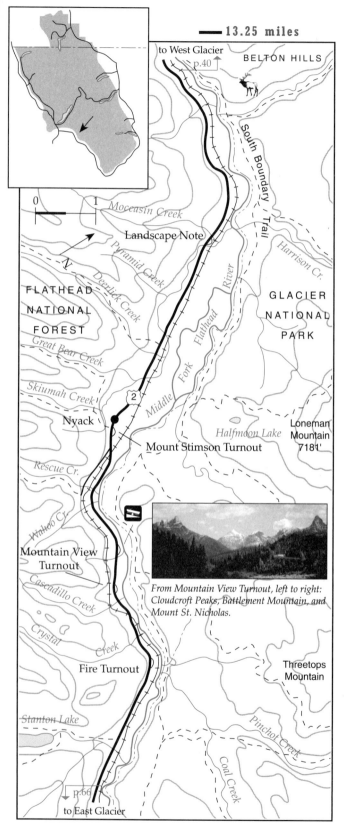

to West Glacier

p.40

BELTON HILLS

South Boundary Trail

Moccasin Creek

Landscape Note

Harrison Cr.

Pyramid Creek

Deerlick Creek

FLATHEAD

NATIONAL

FOREST

GLACIER

NATIONAL

PARK

Flathead River

Great Bear Creek

Skiumah Creek

Middle Fork

0   1

N

Nyack

Halfmoon Lake

Loneman
Mountain
7181'

Mount Stimson Turnout

Rescue Cr.

Waboo Cr.

Mountain View
Turnout

From Mountain View Turnout, left to right:
Cloudcroft Peaks, Battlement Mountain, and
Mount St. Nicholas.

Cascadillo Creek

Crystal

Creek

Threetops
Mountain

Fire Turnout

Stanton Lake

Pinchot Creek

Coal Creek

p.66

to East Glacier

Belton Hills Wildlife Viewing Area: A big fire in 1929 blazed over the Belton Hills north of the river, opening a wide winter range for wildlife. With deep snow covering most of the plants elsewhere, deer and elk come to hills like these to browse the shrubs and dried grasses that are often cleared of snow by wind and sunshine.

Nature Note ■ Flood Plain: Across the tracks and down the slope spreads the gravelly flood plain of the Middle Fork Flathead River, an unstable environment strewn with old snags that the river carried to this spot on the turbulent waters of spring floods. Through the years, changing water levels shift gravel and uproot most plants. The yellow dryad, however, quickly reestablishes itself. Root bacteria supply it with nitrogen, which is in short supply in flood plain soils. Mountains at the head of the valley are (left to right) Blackfoot, 9574 feet, and Thompson, 8527 feet. Loneman Mountain, 7,181 feet stands in the foreground, with a fire lookout near the summit. ■

Mount Stimson: At 10,142 feet, Mount Stimson is one of the highest peaks in Glacier National Park. It was named for Henry Stimson, who visited the Glacier area as early as the 1890s with his friend the conservationist George Bird Grinnell. Stimson served as Secretary of War during World War II.

Mountain View: This long turnout at the gravel banks of the Middle Fork offers the best roadside view of the major peaks at the southwest end of the park. See inset photo, opposite; peaks are (from left to right) Cloudcroft Peaks, Battlement Mountain, and Mount St. Nicholas.

1984 Fire Burn Area: For about a mile, the road passes through an area burned in 1984. Although burned areas can seem desolate at first, regeneration of the forest comes quickly in most burns, providing habitat for some of the park's most popular animals. Ashes return vital nutrients to the soil. Dead trunks attract insects, which in turn feed birds, such as the pileated woodpecker. Sun-loving shrubs, grasses, and wildflowers quickly overrun burned areas, furnishing meals for deer, elk, moose, and bears.

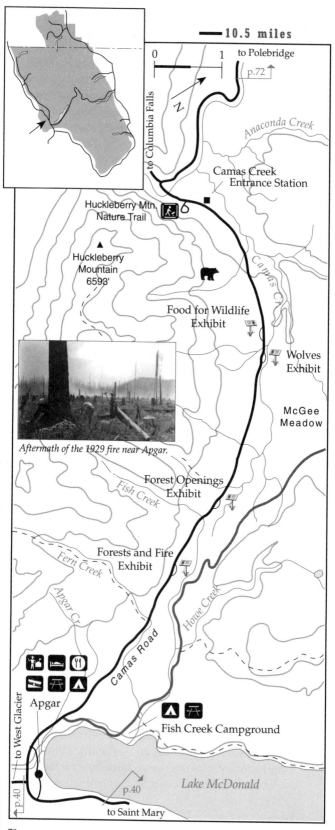

10.5 miles

0   1

to Polebridge
p.72

to Columbia Falls

N

Anaconda Creek

Camas Creek
Entrance Station

Huckleberry Mtn.
Nature Trail

▲
Huckleberry
Mountain
6593'

Food for Wildlife
Exhibit

Camas Cr.

Wolves
Exhibit

McGee
Meadow

Aftermath of the 1929 fire near Apgar.

Fish Creek

Forest Openings
Exhibit

Forests and Fire
Exhibit

Fern Creek

Apgar Cr.

Howe Creek

Camas Road

Apgar

to West Glacier

Fish Creek Campground

p.40

Lake McDonald

p.40

to Saint Mary

70

Camas Road

From Apgar to Polebridge: The forests reflect the aftermath of five major fires: 1929, 1967, 1988, 2001, and 2003. In this area, the 1929 fire wiped out a climax forest of mainly cedar and hemlock. Afterward, a deep forest of lodgepole and larch grew in its place. Subsequent fires burned large sections of the forest and left behind a mosaic of new plant communities of differing ages that provide a variety of habitats for the park animals. Some stands of very tall larch trees survived the fires thanks to thick, fire-resistant bark.

Food for Wildlife Exhibit: One begins to see the effects of the 2001 Moose Fire in the burned trees across the road from the Food for Wildlife Exhibit, and along the high ridge that rises directly over the road. Caused by lightning, the Moose Fire began northwest of the park on August 14 and spread into Glacier on August 31, eventually burning 26,000 acres within the park, including much of the forest around the Camas Creek Entrance Station and sections of the North Fork Valley. Near the entrance station, it also burned a lodgepole forest that had grown in the aftermath of the 1967 Huckleberry Fire, which had blazed through 8,860 acres of timber in eight days.

Just two years after the fire, numerous lodgepole seedlings four to six inches high grow beneath the blackened trunks of their forebears.

Forest Openings Exhibit: This turnout overlooks McGee Meadow, a promising site for spotting elk and deer. The 2003 Robert Fire burned meadow vegetation down to the soil, and yet just weeks afterward new growth had sprouted.

Southwest End Lake McDonald: From this end of Lake McDonald, one clearly sees the effects of the 2003 Robert Fire along Howe Ridge on the lake's west side. The fire started July 23 and burned more than 57,000 acres, mostly in the park. The blaze triggered the evacuation of Apgar and of campgrounds around the lake. Firefighters set backburns to protect structures in Apgar and at Fish Creek campground, which largely explains why one does not see much fire damage in Apgar or along the first few miles of the Camas Road. Then the road skirts about five miles of blackened timber, where the fire burned from forest floor to canopy.

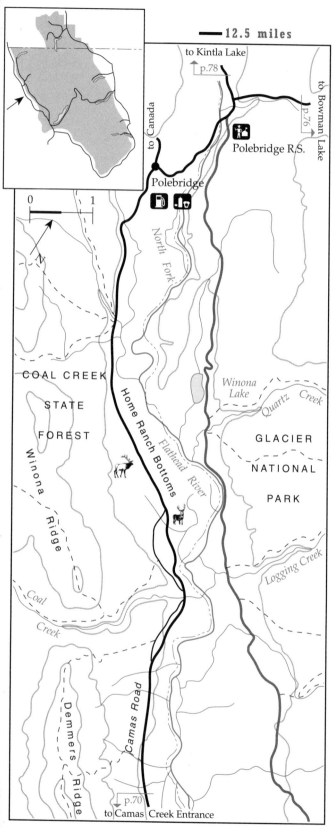

to Kintla Lake

p.78

to Bowman Lake

p.76

Polebridge R.S.

to Canada

Polebridge

North Fork

COAL CREEK

STATE

FOREST

Home Ranch Bottoms

Winona Lake

Quartz Creek

GLACIER

Flathead River

NATIONAL

Winona Ridge

PARK

Logging Creek

Coal Creek

Demmers Ridge

Camas Road

p.70

to Camas Creek Entrance

0   1

N

Outside North Fork Road

1988 Red Bench Fire: As the road approaches Polebridge, effects of the 1988 Red Bench fire become clear. It involved 38,000 acres of trees—burning many, lightly scorching others, and leaving some untouched. As the fire approached Polebridge, firefighters soaked roofs and battled the flames. One died, 19 were injured. Several homesteads and historic structures were destroyed. The stand of dead trees nearby shows how close the flames came to the Polebridge Mercantile, built in 1914. Though it destroys, fire also benefits forests by returning nutrients to the soil and opening the ground to a more diverse assortment of species.

Nature Note ▪ Wolves: Once common in the Glacier area, wolves were hunted in the early years of the park and wiped out. However, during the 1980s, they began to return to and even to den in the North Fork Valley. Two packs now make extensive use of the park, with a total of some 25 wolves roaming the area. ▪

North Fork Valley: Dotted with only a handful of weathered ranch buildings on the west side, this valley is an important habitat for big game. The river and the surrounding mix of marsh, forest, and wide-open prairie grassland attracts deer, elk, moose, black bear, grizzly bear, and wolves.

Lewis Thrust Fault: The valley was created about 60 to 70 million years ago when forces within the Earth raised a broad, east-facing slope about a hundred miles west of the park. Eventually, a huge slab of rock layers 3-to 5-miles thick broke away from the slope and slid eastward for about 40 miles. That slab, thinned by erosion and carved by glaciers, now comprises the mountains of Glacier and Waterton National Parks. When the slab pulled away, gashes tore open behind it. One such gash is now the North Fork Valley, altered by erosion and the movement of an enormous glacier.

Mountain Views: The road runs north through sections of forest opened by the 2001 Moose Fire, occasionally offering sweeping views across the North Fork Valley to the mountains. These are the most comprehensive roadside vistas of the park's west-side ranges.

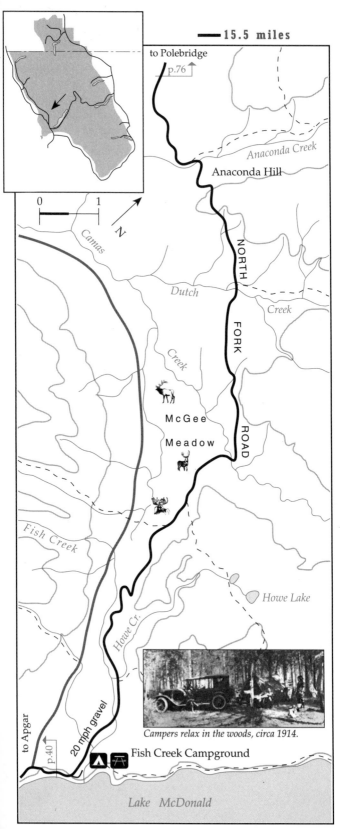

to Polebridge
p.76

15.5 miles

Anaconda Creek

Anaconda Hill

NORTH

Camas

Dutch

Creek

FORK

Creek

McGee

Meadow

ROAD

Fish Creek

Howe Lake

Howe Cr.

Campers relax in the woods, circa 1914.

to Apgar
p.40

20 mph gravel

Fish Creek Campground

Lake McDonald

0   1

N

Inside North Fork Road

Dutch and Anaconda Creeks: The North Fork Valley contains the park's only significant stands of ponderosa pine, an immense tree with thick plates of reddish bark. Look for it on hilltops beyond Dutch and Anaconda Creeks.

Camas Creek: After passing through a short stretch of unburned forest, the road crosses Camas Creek and enters the margin of the 2001 Moose Creek Fire. Here's a wonderful opportunity to compare understory plants in two recently burned forests and to get a sense for the rapid pace of regeneration. Here, just two years ahead of the Robert Fire regeneration, one sees how quickly lodgepole seedlings have established themselves.

At the Camas Creek bridge, swallows dive-bomb for insects, kingfishers whiz by overhead, and woodpeckers can be heard knocking around in the woods. The stream often draws white-tailed deer, which browse the shrubs along the banks and graze the streambed for aquatic plants. Whitetails often stick to small territories of only 40 to 200 acres, enabling them to become familiar with all possible escape routes.

2003 Robert Fire Burn Area: The road passes quickly through a pocket of deep forest giants (western red cedars and hemlocks) then emerges into the sunlit aftermath of the 2003 Robert Fire, which burned more than 57,000 acres during an extremely dry summer and autumn. Here, wide expanses of scorched tree trunks stand high above the ground. With the shade canopy now removed, sun-loving plants have colonized the forest floor. Many of these wildflowers and broad-leafed shrubs make excellent forage for deer and elk. Soon, lodgepole pine seedlings—another sun-loving species—will emerge and begin to form another forest.

Inside North Fork Road: Narrow and often dusty, the rugged Inside North Fork Road twists and turns through some of the most peaceful country in Glacier. This gravel route offers few grand vistas, but does present an intimate tour of the park's forests and the aftermath of three fires that burned large sections of them in 2003, 2001, and 1988. The road cuts north through the forest from the Fish Creek Campground.

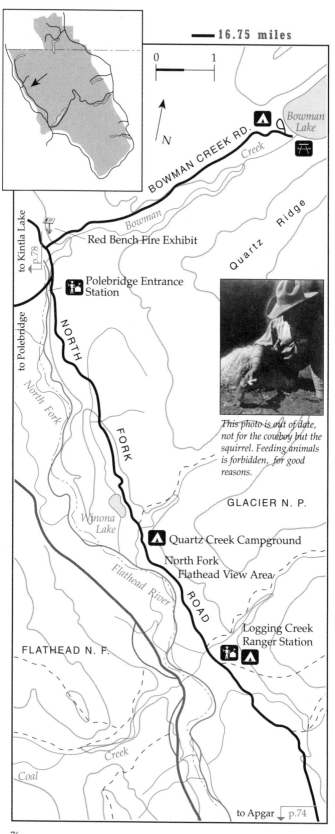

0   1

N

Bowman Lake

BOWMAN CREEK RD.

Creek

Bowman

to Kintla Lake

p.78

Red Bench Fire Exhibit

Polebridge Entrance
Station

to Polebridge

NORTH

North Fork

FORK

Winona Lake

Flathead River

Quartz Ridge

*This photo is out of date,
not for the cowboy but the
squirrel. Feeding animals
is forbidden, for good
reasons.*

GLACIER N. P.

Quartz Creek Campground

North Fork
Flathead View Area

ROAD

Logging Creek
Ranger Station

FLATHEAD N. F.

Creek

Coal

to Apgar   p.74

Bowman Creek Road: The gravel road runs for several miles and climbs out of the fire perimeter to Bowman Lake, which lies at the foot of a ring of mountains.

Roadside Flowers: Easily recognized by their bright pink flowers and prickly stems, shrubs of wild roses grow in profusion along the North Fork Road. After the petals drop, a bright red fruit about the size of a cherry appears. These are rose hips, rich in vitamins and an important food for birds and many mammals, including black bears.

Nature Note ■ Benefits of Fire: Fire maintains a diversity of plant and animal habitats by creating patches of new forest or grassland within the old. Diversity within strengthens the whole forest by breaking up what might otherwise be a uniform woodland vulnerable to disease and infestation. Clearly resilient, the forest began a new cycle of regeneration shortly after the blaze. Within three years the ground lay thick with chest-high fireweed, aspen saplings, snowberries, wild roses, spirea, and lodgepole seedlings. After 15 years, many of those seedlings stood 15 to 20 feet high. ■

Red Bench Fire Perimeter: At the upper end of Winona Lake, the road crosses into the perimeter of the 1988 Red Bench Fire. Touched off by a smoldering snag across the valley, the fire jumped the North Fork and burned irregularly through an area of 38,000 acres. One firefighter was killed, 19 injured, and several homesteads and historic structures were destroyed near Polebridge.

Winona Lake: This shallow lake attracts many types of waterfowl, including loons, as well as large mammals, such as moose. Moose hooves are specially adapted to spread out and keep them from sinking into the mucky bottoms of lakes like this. Their legs are too long for easy grazing on land, so they prefer the aquatic environments. Although moose look awkward, they succeed remarkably well in escaping from wolves. A study of wolves attacking moose on Lake Superior's Isle Royale showed that of 131 moose attacked by wolves, only six were killed. The rest out ran, out swam, or out fought the predators.

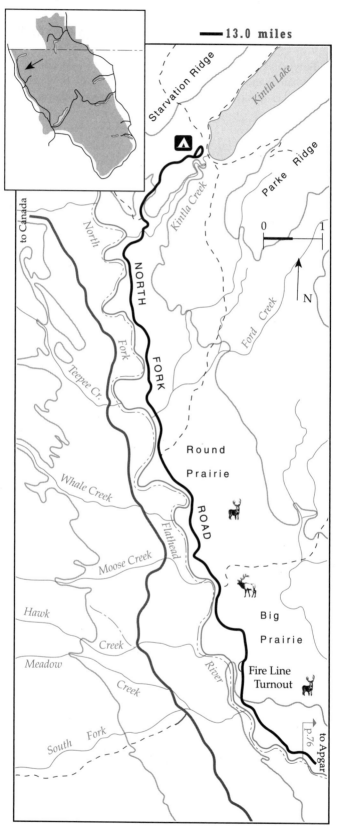

to Canada

Starvation Ridge

Kintla Lake

Parke Ridge

Kintla Creek

NORTH FORK

North Fork

Ford Creek

0   1

N

Teepee Cr.

Round Prairie

ROAD

Whale Creek

Flathead

Moose Creek

Hawk Creek

Big Prairie

Meadow Creek

River

Fire Line Turnout

South Fork

to Apgar
p.76

Kintla Lake: The park's most remote lake for motorists, Kintla is a long, finger lake heavily forested along its northwest shore with larch, Douglas fir, and Engelmann spruce—good black bear habitat. The forest along the southeast shore burned during the 2003 Wedge Canyon Fire.

The lake lies at the feet of Starvation and Parke ridges. The mountain visible at the head of the lake is Long Knife Peak, 9,784 feet high.

Burn Area: Several miles southwest of Kintla Lake, the road moves into a wide area burned by the 2003 Wedge Canyon Fire. Caused by lightning on July 18, the blaze burned for about two months, spreading across more than 53,000 acres and burning seven homes and 29 outbuildings.

Nature Note ■ Howling: Not a melancholy lament but rather a declaration of power, howling among wolves helps mark territory and define the strength of a pack for its neighbors. Wolf packs will attack lone wolves trespassing on their territory and will fight other packs that intrude. Like scent-marking, howling serves as a warning. The more howling voices a pack can raise, the stronger it sounds. Small packs howl only about half as much as medium-sized packs. And a single wolf moving outside its territory rarely howls because raising its voice may invite an attack. ■

Big Prairie: Fires create and reinvigorate grasslands like Big Prairie, which extends for four miles along the banks of the North Fork. The Red Bench Fire moved across this prairie at about 15 mph, burning the grasses to the ground. But since the roots of grasses reach deeper than the scorched surface, they re-emerged from ash-enriched soil none the worse for wear.

Fire Line: At this turnout, a glance to the northwest takes in a view of Big Prairie as it looked before the Red Bench Fire: a lazy vista of grassland bordered by groves of aspen, cottonwood, and bands of dark evergreens. To the southeast lie the results of the fire: a broad reach of grass surrounded by the silvery trunks of dead trees.

Waterton Lakes National Park

Waterton Lakes National Park lies just across the border from Glacier and shares much of the same geology and natural history. Here, as in Glacier, the mountains were part of a vast sheet of ancient sedimentary rock that rose, broke away, and slid eastward. Here, too, the present landscape owes much to the work of immense glaciers that draped the rock walls and filled the main valley to a depth of about 2,000 feet. Deer, elk, moose, black bears, grizzlies, bighorn sheep, mountain goats, cougars, and coyotes all live here as well as in Glacier.

Still, there are differences between the parks. Waterton's mountains no longer hold glaciers. Peaks in the U.S. park do. In a large paddock north of Waterton, visitors will find a small bison herd that the park maintains as a reminder of times past. Not so near Glacier. Also, Waterton lies farther off the beaten track and strikes most visitors as a quieter park— as long as they can find a place out of the wind.

Waterton is famous for its wind, which averages about 20 mph, frequently gusts to 75 mph and has been known to reach 100 mph. While the Prince of Wales Hotel was under construction in 1927, a fierce blast slid the completed timber frame eight inches along the foundation. The building has never been square since. Wind has a strong drying influence. It discourages plant growth in some areas, stunts trees and, in the winter, blows off snow so wildlife can feed on exposed grasses.

Opposite: Early visitors pause along the shoulder of the Akamina Parkway.

In Waterton, moist Pacific air battles with frigid arctic weather. The Pacific influence usually dominates, moderating winter temperatures. On average, Waterton is one of the warmest spots in Alberta during the winter. It is also the wettest spot in Alberta year-round.

The unique climate accounts in part for the rich and widely varied plant life that Waterton enjoys. A total of some 1,300 species of plants, including 800 different flowers, grows in the park. These plants support about 250 species of birds, 60 mammals, and 10 reptiles and amphibians.

The park is laid out in three major valleys. The main valley encloses the chain of three Waterton Lakes, which were named for an eccentric British naturalist who never set foot in the park but probably would have enjoyed a visit. The lakes begin with Upper Waterton Lake, ringed with high peaks. They run out to the prairie east of the park, and terminate in shallow Maskinonge Lake. Every autumn, the lower lakes clog with waterfowl headed south on one of two major flyways that run alongside the park.

The Red Rock Canyon Parkway follows Blakiston Creek toward South Kootenay Pass, an ancient route followed by native people traveling through the mountains from buffalo hunts on the eastern prairies. The valley ends at a gorge, where turquoise water runs over bright red rock. Black bear, bighorn sheep, and deer frequent the area.

John George "Kootenai" Brown became the park's first superintendent in 1911.

The third valley, capped by rock-ringed Cameron Lake, stretches from Cameron Falls into the park's highest forest. The road, called the Akamina Parkway, skirts a deep gorge, then climbs into a wide, U-shaped valley. Many deer live in the valley, and grizzly bears are sometimes spotted on the avalanche slopes at the south end of Cameron Lake.

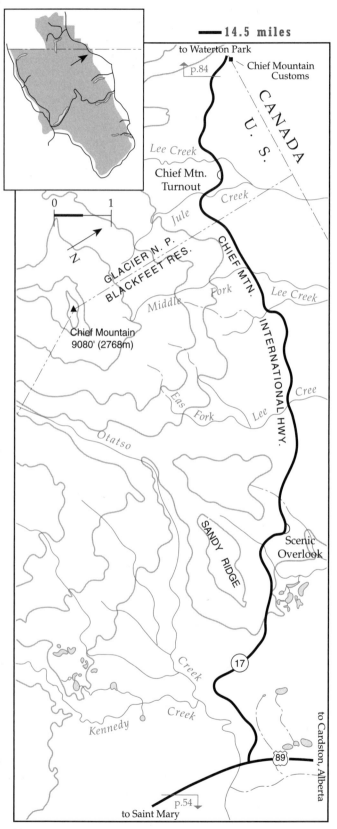

— 14.5 miles

to Waterton Park

Chief Mountain
Customs

p.84

C A N A D A
U. S.

Lee Creek

Chief Mtn.
Turnout

Creek

Jule

GLACIER N. P.
BLACKFEET RES.

CHIEF MTN.

Pork

Lee Creek

Middle

Chief Mountain
9080' (2768m)

INTERNATIONAL HWY.

Eas

Fork

Lee

Cree

Otatso

SANDY RIDGE

Scenic
Overlook

17

Creek

to Cardston, Alberta

Creek

Kennedy

89

p.54

to Saint Mary

Chief Mountain International Highway

Chief Mountain International Highway: This pleasant road linking Glacier and Waterton Lakes National Parks takes its name from Chief Mountain, the isolated, stump-like peak that juts above the gentle hills to the west. The road opened to motorists in 1935, three years after Glacier and Waterton Lakes became the world's first international peace park. The sprawling, broad-backed mountain to the left of Chief is Yellow Mountain (elev. 8966 feet), which ends in a tidy pyramid called Sherburne Peak (elev. 8578 feet).

Chief Mountain: For generations, native people have favored this impressive tower of ancient rock as a site for vision quests because it is thought to be the home of the Thunder Bird and perhaps the Wind Spirit. During such a quest, the vision seeker finds an isolated spot, calls upon the spirits for a dream of power, and waits—often for days, and often without food or water. Among the Blackfeet, the spirit traditionally came in the form of an animal or some natural force, such as thunder, which gave some of its power to the seeker. It also taught the seeker to tap this power with songs, face painting, and rituals involving symbols of power contained in a medicine bundle.

The peak, elevation 9,080 feet, is the easternmost extension of the Lewis Thrust Fault Block.

Scenic Overlook: From the top of this rise, the land slopes away to the northeast and then runs for hundreds of miles across the Great Plains. Out there, on the undulating grasslands, bison once drifted in immense herds. The shaggy animals sustained native tribes (most recently the Blackfeet) with food, clothing, tools, and shelter for thousands of years. Today, cattle graze the land, mostly on ranches owned by the Blackfeet.

Nature Note ■ Landscape in Transition: As the road makes a broad, southerly curve, it passes through both prairie and forest landscape. Here, grassland gives way to groves of aspen, which thrive wherever water tends to collect—in ravines, glens, hollows, and throughout the bottomland irrigated by Kennedy and Otatso Creeks. Hawks glide over the meadows and hillocks in search of ground squirrels, mice, and voles. Coyotes patrol the same territory afoot. White-tailed deer hide in the groves during the day and take to the meadows at dusk. ■

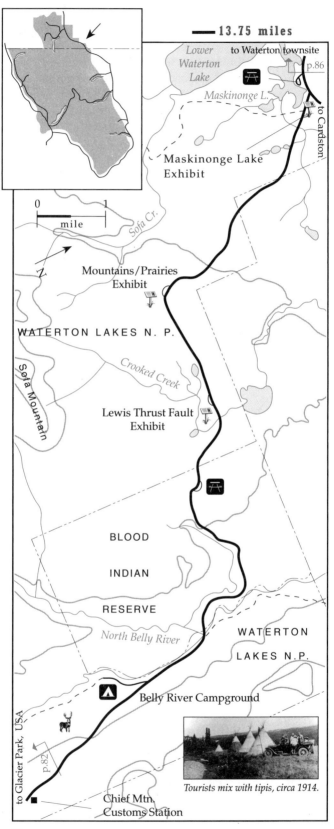

13.75 miles

Lower Waterton Lake

to Waterton townsite

p.86

to Cardston

Maskinonge L.

Maskinonge Lake Exhibit

0   1
mile

Sofa Cr.

Mountains/Prairies Exhibit

WATERTON LAKES N. P.

Crooked Creek

Sofa Mountain

Lewis Thrust Fault Exhibit

BLOOD

INDIAN

RESERVE

North Belly River

WATERTON

LAKES N. P.

Belly River Campground

to Glacier Park, USA

p.82

Chief Mtn. Customs Station

Tourists mix with tipis, circa 1914.

Maskinonge Lake Exhibit: This shallow lake, averaging just 1.5 feet deep, is perhaps the richest aquatic environment in the park. Its relatively warm waters support an abundant growth of pondweeds, sedges, rushes, and cattails. One plant, the carnivorous bladderwort, catches prey in trapdoor bladders it trails in the water. When a hapless insect larva swims too close, the trapdoor opens, water rushes into the hollow chamber and sucks in the larva. When it blooms above water in June and July, bladderwort looks a bit like a yellow snapdragon. Great blue herons stalk the fringes of the lake, nabbing leopard frogs and minnows. Garter snakes slither through the rushes in search of tadpoles. Muskrats yank up the aquatic vegetation and drag it back to their lodges, where they can chew on it in safety. Lots of muskrats never make it back to the nest, though, since they make favorite meals for mink and great horned owls. In the late evening, mule deer, white-tailed deer, and elk often venture onto the reedy flats, and bats dart overhead, catching insects.

Lewis Overthrust Exhibit: Here, a park information sign identifies Sofa Mountain as part of the leading edge of the Lewis Overthrust (a.k.a. the Lewis Thrust Fault), that vast slab of ancient sedimentary rock that composes the mountains of Waterton and Glacier National Parks.

Burned trees along the flanks of Sofa Mountain and in the bottomlands near this exhibit mark the Sofa Mountain Fire of 1998.

Blood Reserve: A few miles down the road from the border, a sign identifies the Blood Indian Reserve, which begins just the other side of Belly River. The Blood are one of three tribes that make up the Blackfeet people. During buffalo days, they joined forces with the Piegan and Northern Blackfoot tribes to become the strongest military power on the northwest plains.

International Border: Although people must stop here to take official notice of the border, eagles, deer, bear, and other wildlife do not recognize such abstract divisions of land. Therefore, as befits an international peace park, the U.S. and Canadian park services try whenever possible to manage the ecosystem as if it did not lie in separate nations.

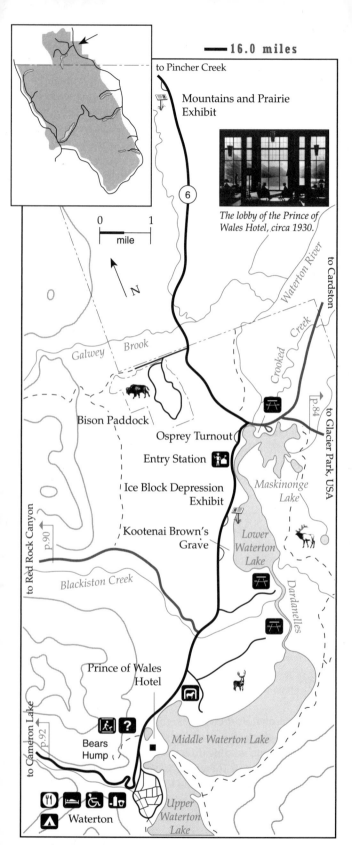

to Pincher Creek

Mountains and Prairie
Exhibit

6

The lobby of the Prince of
Wales Hotel, circa 1930.

Waterton River

to Cardston

Crooked Creek

Galwey Brook

0   1
mile

N

p.84

to Glacier Park, USA

Bison Paddock

Osprey Turnout

Entry Station

Maskinonge
Lake

Ice Block Depression
Exhibit

Kootenai Brown's
Grave

Lower
Waterton
Lake

to Red Rock Canyon

p.90

Blackiston Creek

Dardanelles

Prince of Wales
Hotel

to Cameron Lake

p.92

Bears
Hump

Middle Waterton Lake

Waterton

Upper
Waterton
Lake

Waterton Valley

Mountains and Prairie Exhibit: This excellent exhibit offers a sweeping view of the undulating prairie as it makes its last run toward the mountains. A sign helps visitors identify prominent peaks.

> **Nature Note** ■ Beaver: Carpeted with groves of aspen and various poplars, the broad, marshy bottomlands north of the park make a fine home for beaver. The largest rodent in North America, beaver can weigh more than 75 pounds and have been known to fell trees 4 feet in diameter. The wetlands they create with their ponds and canals furnish important habitat for waterfowl, amphibians, and other mammals including moose, muskrat, and otters. Wetlands also control erosion and filter sediments. ■

Bison Paddock: A small herd of bison live in a large, fenced enclosure just a quarter mile west of the road. Weighing as much as a ton and standing as high as 6 feet, the bison is the largest land animal in North America. Once numbering roughly 50 million, bison had a profound effect on the prairie ecosystem. By cropping, digesting, and excreting grasses, they played a major role in building up the very soil they thundered across.

Osprey Nest: The large tangle of twigs and branches on the stand in the marsh is an osprey nest. From spring to autumn, they raise their young and fish the waters of Maskinonge and Lower Waterton Lakes.

Kootenai Brown's Grave: John George "Kootenai" Brown —former British Army officer, gold miner, sheriff, pony express rider, buffalo hunter, wolf hunter, and one-time captive of Sitting Bull—settled nearby in 1879. He ranched, fished, hunted, guided, and extolled the virtues of Waterton Valley. He became the park's first superintendent in 1911 and died in 1916. His grave lies in the aspens down the hill.

Prince of Wales Hotel: The Great Northern Railway opened this lovely Swiss-style hotel in 1927 as a stopover for rich visitors making bus and horse tours of Glacier. Open to all, the hotel offers a fine, wind-free vista of the upper lake and its surrounding peaks.

From Prince of Wales Hotel

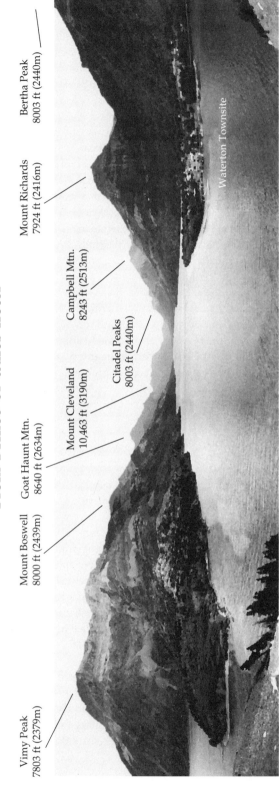

Vimy Peak
7803 ft (2379m)

Mount Boswell
8000 ft (2439m)

Goat Haunt Mtn.
8640 ft (2634m)

Mount Cleveland
10,463 ft (3190m)

Citadel Peaks
8003 ft (2440m)

Campbell Mtn.
8243 ft (2513m)

Mount Richards
7924 ft (2416m)

Bertha Peak
8003 ft (2440m)

Waterton Townsite

Reading the Landscape

■ **Mountain Building** ■ The strata of the mountains ringing Upper Waterton Lake began forming 1.5 billion years ago when this area lay along the shifting coastline of an ancient sea. Sediments ran off a vast ramp of land, collecting on the seabed and tidal flats. Much of the sediment contained iron, which rusted red when deposited on tidal flats and turned grayish green when deposited under water. Mats of blue-green algae lived, died, and fossilized in beds of limestone. Lava poured over the seabed and intruded under pressure between layers of limestone.

This process continued for hundreds of millions of years as life evolved from algal slime to dinosaurs and primates. Roughly 60-to 70-million-years ago, the earth's crust began rising to the west in a colossal uplift that eventually formed the Rockies. The mountains here were part of a slab of rock about the size of Glacier-Waterton parks that broke loose and moved nearly 40 miles along the Lewis Thrust Fault.

■ **Glaciation** ■ Though glaciers no longer exist in Waterton Lakes National Park, the effect of the last great ice age on the park's landscape is clear. Some 10,000 years ago, a glacier 2,000 feet thick and 15 miles long gouged out the broad, U-shaped valley of the Waterton Lakes chain. Smaller, tributary glaciers joined it from the valleys between Vimy Peak and Mount Boswell, Campbell Mountain and Mount Richards, Mount Richards and Bertha Peak. The glacier slowed at the Bosporous, where a ridge of limestone extended from Bear's Hump to Vimy Peak. As it paused to surmount this obstacle, the moving ice dug deeply into the trough that would become the upper lake. When the glacier receded, it split over what remained of the ridge and stranded an enormous block of ice. which melted to form a lower lake. This lake divided as debris from the Blakiston Valley formed an alluvial fan. The town of Waterton stands on a similar fan.

■ **Upper Waterton Lake** ■ With a maximum of 487 feet, Upper Waterton Lake is the deepest lake in the Canadian Rockies. Its frigid, oxygen-rich waters support trout, whitefish, sculpin, northern pike, suckers, and ling cod.

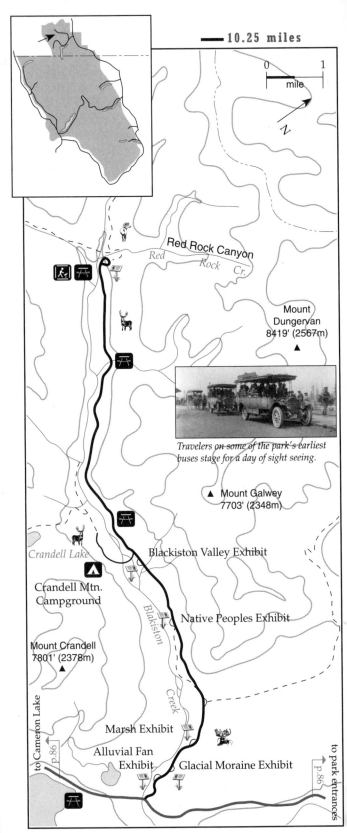

10.25 miles

0   1
mile

N

Red Rock Canyon

Red Rock Cr.

Mount Dungervan
8419' (2567m)

Travelers on some of the park's earliest
buses stage for a day of sight seeing.

▲ Mount Galwey
7703' (2348m)

Crandell Lake

Blackiston Valley Exhibit

Crandell Mtn.
Campground

Native Peoples Exhibit

Blackiston

Mount Crandell
7801' (2378m)

Creek

to Cameron Lake   p.86

Marsh Exhibit

Alluvial Fan
Exhibit   Glacial Moraine Exhibit

to park entrances   p.86

Red Rock Parkway

Red Rock Canyon: A testament to the power of water, Red Rock Canyon was cut out of bright red mudstone over a period of thousands of years by a crystalline stream. The self-guiding trail along the gorge explains the forces of erosion. The Purcell Sill, an ancient infusion of lava between layers of limestone, runs like a ribbon across the face of Anderson Peak. Bighorn sheep often stroll the parking lot. Please don't feed them.

Crandell Campground: As in most of the valley, the vegetation surrounding this camp divides into two distinct zones. South-facing slopes catch more sun and dry out quickly, making it tough for any trees to grow. North-facing slopes hold moisture longer, enabling lodgepole pine and Douglas fir to prosper.

This division also extends to animals. Ground squirrels on the south keep a sharp eye out for hawks while foraging the prairie for plants, insects, and the occasional mouse. Across the valley, red squirrels try to steer clear of pine martens and owls while scrambling through the trees hunting up conifer seeds, insects, and the occasional baby bird.

Blakiston Valley: People have travelled through this broad valley of prairie and mountain landscapes for at least 8,000 years. It led native people west over South Kootenay Pass to areas in Montana where they could obtain obsidian for the points of spears and arrows. For those living west, it led to the buffalo plains.

Marsh Exhibit: A sign explains how beaver activity and the shifting flow of Blakiston Creek created this backwater slough. Moose occasionally feed here.

Glacial Moraine Exhibit: An interpretive sign describes how glaciers formed the rolling landscape underlying this broad reach of oatgrass, fescue, and wildflowers. Rodents thrive here, feeding off seeds, flowers, insects and, in some cases, each other.

One of the most common, the deer mouse, is exceptional among mammals for the care male parents provide their offspring. Excluded from the nest at birth, the male later returns to help groom the young and lead them on foraging trips. Like other prairie rodents, they fall prey to coyotes and raptors. Only five percent of deer mice live past the first year.

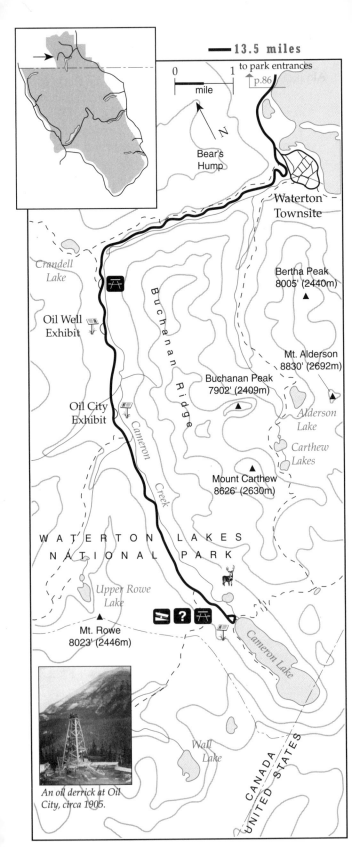

0
1
mile

N

to park entrances
p.86

Bear's
Hump

Waterton
Townsite

Crandell
Lake

Bertha Peak
8005' (2440m) ▲

Oil Well
Exhibit

Mt. Alderson
8830' (2692m) ▲

Buchanan Peak
7902' (2409m) ▲

Alderson
Lake

B
u
c
h
a
n
a
n

R
i
d
g
e

Carthew
Lakes

Oil City
Exhibit

C
a
m
e
r
o
n

C
r
e
e
k

Mount Carthew
8626' (2630m) ▲

W A T E R T O N   L A K E S
N A T I O N A L   P A R K

Upper Rowe
Lake

Cameron
Lake

Mt. Rowe
8023' (2446m) ▲

Wall
Lake

C A N A D A
U N I T E D   S T A T E S

An oil derrick at Oil City, circa 1905.

Alabama Parkway

Akamina Parkway: From Emerald Bay picnic area, the road climbs toward Bertha Peak, with its funneling network of avalanche chutes, and then veers sharply toward the gnarly cliffs of Bear's Hump. The folded, almost swirled layers of rock give one a sense of the immense forces that lifted and moved these mountains millions of years ago.

Nature Note ■ Changing shape of Cameron Valley: As it skirts the base of Mount Crandell, the road runs beside a gorge cut into 1.5-billion-year-old limestone by Cameron Creek. If it feels a bit more confining here than in Waterton Valley, it should. This is a good example of a stream-cut, V-shaped valley. Most of the valleys in the park looked this way until glaciers broadened them. After making a big, southwest curve, the road emerges onto the spacious floor of a broad, U-shaped valley. The glacier that carved this portion of Cameron Valley could not make the sharp turn at Mount Crandell. Instead, it flowed between Crandell and Ruby Ridge, creating the depression where hikers will find Crandell Lake. ■

Oil Marker: A white obelisk marks the remnants of western Canada's first producing oil well: a thick cylinder of rusted steel with blocks of weathered wood still bolted to it. The well produced, but the pool dried up quickly and so did its accompanying boomtown.

Cameron Lake: Set beneath a cirque of cliffs 2,000 feet high, much of Cameron Lake is surrounded by a mature forest of subalpine fir, Engelmann spruce, larch, and whitebark pine. These trees may not look old, but many have grown here for 300 to 400 years. A short growing season explains their modest size. Along the trail on the lake's west side, visitors will find bear grass, a tall stalk topped by a 6-inch spray of tiny white flowers.

Both black bear and grizzly live around Cameron Lake. Black bears spend most of their time in the forest, eating buds, roots, grubs, and mice. Grizzlies tend to stay higher, digging for roots and ground squirrels in the alpine meadows. In autumn, both gorge themselves with berries that grow on avalanche slopes at the south end of the lake.

Index

Further Reading

Alden, Peter, and Grassy. *National Audubon Society Field Guide to the Rocky Mountain States.* Alfred A. Knopf, 1998.

Alt, David, and Hyndman. *Roadside Geology of Montana.* Mountain Press, 1986, 1991, 2003.

Ewers, John C. *The Blackfeet: Raiders on the Northwestern Plains.* University of Oklahoma Press, 1958, 2003.

Glacier Natural History Ass'n. *Short Hikes and Strolls in Glacier National Park.* Glacier Natural History Association, 1993.

Glacier Natural History Ass'n. *Hiker's Guide to Glacier National Park.* Glacier Natural History Ass'n, 1996.

Kershaw, MacKinnon, and Pojar. *Plants of the Rocky Mountains.* Lone Pine Publishing, 1993, 1998.

Raup, Omer B. et al. *Geology Along Going-to-the-Sun Road Glacier National Park, Montana.* Glacier Natural History Association, 1983, 2003.

Phillips, H. Wayne. *Central Rocky Mountain Wildflowers.* Falcon Publishing, 1999.

Schmidt, Thomas. *National Geographic's Guide to the Lewis and Clark Trail.* National Geographic Society, 1998, 2002.

Schmidt, Thomas and Jeremy. *The Saga of Lewis and Clark: Into the Uncharted West.* DK Publishing, 1999.

Thomas Schmidt fell for the Rocky Mountains as a boy, while spending summers in the West with his family. He is the author of four books about the human and natural history of the West and has contributed to many other books published by the National Geographic Society.

He lives in Bozeman, Montana, with his wife, Terese, and their two children, Pat and Colleen.

Wendy Baylor and Jeremy Schmidt,
  Computer composition and design for original edition
Wendy Baylor, *Maps*
Jocelyn Slack, *Illustrations*
Glenbow Archives, *Historic photos on pp. 80, 81, 92*
Glacier National History Association, *all other photos*

National Geographic Travel Books:

Caroline Hickey, *Project Manager*
Cinda Rose, *Art Director*
Bea Jackson, *Cover Design*

Copyright © 1992, 1994, 2000, and 2004 by Thomas Schmidt

Library of Congress Cataloging-in-Publication Data

Schmidt, Thomas, 1959-
National Geographic Glacier and Waterton Lakes National Parks
road guide : the essential guide for motorists / by Thomas Schmidt.
p. cm.
Rev. ed. of: Glacier and Waterton Lakes National Parks road guide :
the essential guide for motorists. 3rd ed. 2000.
Includes bibliographical references and index.
ISBN 0-7922-6637-4
1. Glacier National Park (Mont.)--Guidebooks. 2. Automobile travel
--Montana--Glacier National Park--Guidebooks. 3. Waterton Lakes
National Park (Alta.)--Guidebooks. 4. Automobile travel--Alberta—
Waterton Lakes National Park--Guidebooks. I. Title: Glacier and
Waterton Lakes National Parks road guide. II. Schmidt,Thomas,
1959- Glacier and Waterton Lakes National Parks road guide. III.

National Geographic Society (U.S.) IV. Title.
F737.G5S36 2004   2003022221
917.86'5204--dc22